Contact

The Practical Science of Hearing from God

By Dr. David Stine

Companion to *The Experiment—40 Days of Hearing God's Voice Workbook*

ISBN-13: 978-1517033767
ISBN-10: 1517033764

Metro Publishing:
1200 N. Fayette St, Alexandria, VA 22314
Phone: 703.229.4488
dcmetro.org

Quantity sales: Special discounts are available on quantity purchases by corporations, associations, and others. For details, contact the publisher at the address above.

Printed in the United States of America

Editorial Services: David Yeazell, dayeazell@juno.com

Graphic Formatting and Front Cover Design: Jonelly Sharp and Zanna Roden

ENDORSEMENTS

In a culture where there can be many competing "voices" in our lives, the voice that carries the greatest weight can only come from God. God desires relational intimacy with all of us and this can only be cultivated by learning to listen and recognize His voice. David Stine has written a powerful and highly practical book that de-mystifies this process. This is a must-read for everyone!

Stovall Weems
Lead Pastor of Celebration Church in Jacksonville, Florida
Author of *Living the God-First Life*

Having had the privilege of knowing David and his wife personally for over 20 years, I can say that David Stine knows what it means to walk with God. His life is an example of someone who seeks the Lord with all of his heart. This book will help resurrect your walk with God as David uses his testimony and experiences to help you hear God's voice in your life. David is able to make complicated ideas understandable so that we can apply them to our lives. This book will help you to commit to seeking God first and everything else will be added to you.

Pastor Joe Champion
Lead Pastor of Celebration Church in Austin, Texas
Author of *Rocked: How to Respond When Life's Circumstances Rock You to Your Core*

David Stine is a gifted leader, a humble servant, and someone who hears from God. If you're struggling to hear God's voice, this book is for you. It'll help you hear God more clearly, more consistently.

Mark Batterson
Lead Pastor of National Community Church in Washington D.C., New York Times Best-Selling Author of *The Circle Maker: Praying Circles Around Your Biggest Dreams and Greatest Fears*

There is nothing more elemental to Christian pursuit or more essential to Christian living than hearing the voice of God. With equal parts good theology and good sense, David Stine's crack at this age-old question demystifies a cluttered subject and offers refreshing, practical help. With the intellectual honesty of a scientist, the care of a pastor, and the zeal of a man who lives this stuff, he helps us relate to a God who is both mystical and rational.

Rob Brendle
Lead Pastor of Denver United Church in Denver, Colorado
Author of *In the Meantime: The Practice of Proactive Waiting*

David Stine's new book, *Contact: The Practical Science of Hearing from God* is more than just a book; it's a step-by-step training manual in how to spend time with the Lord. Much like learning a foreign language, learning to hear the voice of God is a skill that can be acquired through teaching, instruction, and practice. David has done a masterful job of communicating in a simple and understandable way the practical steps to hearing God's voice, and what to do when He does speak. The foundational revelation in this book will open the door to new dimensions in your life. I highly recommend it!

Kris Vallotton
Associate Pastor at Bethel Church in Redding, California
Author of *The Supernatural Ways of Royalty: Discovering Your Rights and Privileges of Being a Son or Daughter of God*

This book is not theory; it is the reality of a man who has tested it personally and vocationally; finding it both true and trustworthy. Reading Dr. David's personal milestone stories will give you hope and help to upgrade your own story of God's blueprint for your life and ministry. The good news is that the author makes the complicated simple without dumbing down the power and life change of "a Word in season" in your own life.

Because I have watched this book work itself through the life of the author as my student, ministry staff, and now as an overseer for this esteemed and sought after church planter, I can attest to its truthfulness and fruitfulness. On the other side of this exciting read you will have a hunger and thirst for hearing and obeying our Abba Father, who calls you by name and leads you out into this courageous adventure of trusting His daily voice to you.

Dr. Joseph Umidi
Interim Dean of Divinity and Executive Vice President of Regent University in Virginia Beach, Virginia
Author of *Transformational Coaching*

ACKNOWLEDGMENTS

I would first and foremost like to thank **Jesus.** In the past twenty years of walking with you, I have learned there is no more worthwhile pursuit than knowing you and following your voice. I am who I am because of you. I would also like to thank:

Taryn—From the first time I met you and you told me that you wanted to "do something great for God," I knew you were the one I wanted with me on this journey. You have helped me become a better man, a better leader, and a better father. After thirteen years of marriage, I am even more in love with you; and, I believe we are about to walk into our best season as we continue to follow God's voice together.

Isaac, Josiah, Asher, and Karis—I pray that you too would walk in this adventure of learning to hear and follow God's voice. You are my favorite legacy, and I can't wait to see what God does through each of your lives as you say "yes' to Him. I love you so much!

My Parents—Dad, I watched you kneel beside your bed every night modeling a life of prayer; and Mom, your love for God and for me helped me find Him. I would not be who I am today without both of your influences or the godly legacy you passed down to me.

My Grandfather—I watched you study your Bible, while I studied your life, and you made me want to know the God that you knew. You taught me about hearing the voice of God, and in many ways inspired the journey that led to this book. I can't wait to see you again.

Julie Reams—Thank you for all your help with every step of the journey towards my first book becoming published. You became my Baruch (Jeremiah 36:32) as my scribe and editor, but most importantly as my friend. Your friendship is such a gift to Taryn and me.

DC Metro Launch Team—Thanks for following the voice of the Lord to embark upon the adventure of planting DC Metro Church with Taryn and me. We appreciate your support and belief in the vision before it was a reality more than you know.

DC Metro Staff and Family—We would not be where we are today if you had not chosen to invest your lives in this vision of building a God-first culture throughout the DC Metro area. We are thankful for each of you, and we are excited to follow God's voice with you!

CONTENTS

FREE RESOURCES

Send an email to resources@contactexperiment.com or visit http://ContactExperiment.com/resources to receive these bonuses:

- "Using Contact in Your Daily Life": An exclusive interview with Dr. Stine on how he applies the principles of *Contact* on a daily basis, and how you can too.

- "Contact, The Practical Science of Hearing from God": Exclusive video sermon presented by Dr. Stine.

FOREWORD

This is a book for at least two kinds of people. First, people wise enough to want to discover *keys* that open doors to meaning in life and effectiveness in its pursuit. Second, people honest enough with themselves to admit they need a map when they are navigating a new territory.

To read this book will be both an exciting adventure and a profitable discovery. The author's introductory framework—to present a *scientific* grid as a means of distilling a *spiritual* reality and making it practical—is decidedly and skillfully achieved.

To write this foreword mandated a careful coverage since the very nature of the words *Hearing God's Voice* conjure up the potential of either discerning workable wisdom for a lifelong journey, or stumbling blindly onto a pathway of gullibility, presumption and confusion about God, His Word, His ways...and His voice.

As a shepherd of souls—a pastor for nearly fifty years—I've learned a great deal about people, a good deal of God's Word, and a lot about God himself—His heart for us all, His Son given to redeem and teach us and His Spirit to enlighten our souls, guide our minds and whisper *reminders* and *refining course corrections* as we journey with the Father.

David Stine's work and pastoral sensitivities flavor this entire book and his grounding in God's Word provides its strong foundation and practical viability.

I could not be more grateful than I am now to point to a tool for building life or a rod to take in as a means of balance as you traverse day to day life. Read it—and move forward toward a goal of learning the joys and blessing that transcends the trials and lessons life inevitably brings us all.

Proceed if you will: you *will* be profited, your heart instructed, your mind sharpened, and your feet secured on your way as you listen to God's voice—in His Word.

Jack W. Hayford
Chancellor of The Kings University in Southlake, Texas
Pastor Emeritus of The Church of the Way in Van Nuys, CA
Author of *The Reward of Worship* and *Prayer: Invading the Impossible*

PART ONE

CONTACT

There is a great Sci-fi movie that came out in 1997 called *Contact*. Based on a Carl Sagan novel by the same name, the movie follows the main character, Ellie Arroway, from childhood to her career as a research scientist with the SETI program (Search for Extraterrestrial Intelligence). The pre-teen Ellie—later Dr. Arroway—has an insatiable desire to make contact with the outside world. What starts as reaching outside of her childhood home through a CB radio, develops into a life devoted to searching for life outside our solar system.

In the opening scenes in the movie, Ellie excitedly makes contact on her CB radio with someone in Florida, which leads to questions about the possibility of making contact with the different stars she had viewed in her telescope. Eventually, as an adult, her search for contact from world's beyond pays off, as she receives a series of communications from the distant star Vega.

One of the most gripping scenes takes place early in the movie after Ellie's father dies. In the midst of the tragedy, while family and friends are downstairs socializing after the funeral, Ellie is up in her bedroom, seated in front of the CB radio, attempting to make contact: "Dad, are you there? This is Ellie. Dad, are you there?"

I called this book *Contact: The Practical Science of Hearing from God* because I believe, as humans, we all want to make contact with our heavenly Father—God—and hear and recognize His voice. Many of the world's religions are like Ellie's CB radio, where we call out to God, "Dad, are you there?" hoping that perhaps we will get some kind of reply—an assurance that He exists and is somehow interested in our lives—even if it's only a scratchy, faint hum.

As believers I am convinced that God wants to make contact with us even more than we want to hear from Him. Instead of a faint, indistinguishable hum, He wants to speak clearly to His people.

God speaking to us is meant to be normal Christianity, but unfortunately it is not for many. According to a recent study by George Barna, more than eighty percent of Americans pray during a typical week, but only thirty-eight percent are certain that Jesus talks back to them in a personal and relevant way, while an additional twenty-one percent are only somewhat certain that God speaks to them personally.[1]

The most common question I am asked as a pastor is, "How do I hear from God?"

There is so much confusion, uncertainty, and ambiguity related to this subject, but I believe God wants to bring clarity so that conversational intimacy can be developed between Him and any believer. John 10:27 expresses that thought clearly: "My sheep listen to my voice; I know them, and they follow Me." This is an invitation for all believers to listen to and hear God's voice.

The longer I have walked in relationship with Him, the more confident I have become that He wants to make contact: speak specifically and frequently to each of us. So if He wants to speak and we want to hear, the million-dollar question is: how do we position our lives to make that contact and hear clearly from God? I do not consider myself to be an expert in this area, and I will share stories in this book where I missed God's voice in important ways, but I have learned invaluable truths and practical applications that have absolutely revolutionized my walk with God and my ability to hear from Him. I have also found that the biggest hindrance to hearing from God is me—not God.

So many believers either do not believe that they have a significant role to play in hearing from God or they do not understand what they can do to increase their ability to discern His voice. Instead they buy into the lie that God does not speak to them or that there is something wrong with them that keeps them from making contact.

The reality for most believers is that they just need some coaching on how they can position themselves to hear from Him and on how to recognize His voice. There is a concept I call the ministry of Eli. Eli was High Priest in the Jewish temple and was instrumental in helping the young boy Samuel (who later became a prophet) recognize the voice of God speaking to him. I want this book to become like the ministry of Eli to you. I have benefited greatly from being coached in this area by other pastors, mentors, and friends, and I am excited to share with you what I have learned along the way.

I am confident that as you put into practice what I teach in this book, you too will make contact and hear Him. If you already hear from God, I believe this book will help you grow in your ability to discern His voice even more clearly and to teach others how they can grow in hearing from God.

THE PRACTICAL SCIENCE

Science has been described as God allowing man to discover the secret workings of His incredible creation. For Dr. Arroway, although the search was not based on a faith in God, it was based on discovering whatever was *out there* in the unknown universe. I believe God wants to help man discover not only the secret workings of His natural creation, but also the secret workings of His supernatural realm, including hearing His voice.

The term <u>practical science</u> is defined as "the discipline of applying specific knowledge to practical problems." It is the synthesis of these two concepts that coveys the heart of this book.

Contact: The Practical Science of Hearing from God is written to help believers discover and apply specific knowledge to the practical dilemma of wanting to hear clearly from Him so that we can experience more depth in our relationship with Him. Although hearing from God cannot be reduced to an exact science in the typical connotation of the word, I believe there are specific action steps to take and important components that we need to include in the *formula* of our lives to increase our propensity and frequency of hearing from Him. We live in the natural realm, but as believers we are also called to seek out the supernatural realm through a vibrant relationship with the living God. So how do we practically do this?

THE SCIENTIFIC METHOD

Do you remember the scientific method from high school or college days? Since I am causing many of you to dig deep into the recesses of your mind, let me give you a little refresher. The scientific method is a body of techniques for investigating phenomena, acquiring new knowledge, or correcting and integrating previous knowledge. It includes the following six steps:

Step One: Ask a Question

Step Two: Do Background Research

Step Three: Construct a Hypothesis

Step Four: Test Your Hypothesis by Doing an Experiment

Step Five: Analyze Your Data and Draw a Conclusion

Step Six: Communicate Your Results

Although it is not a perfect correlation, when we apply the scientific method to hearing the voice of God, we come up with the following:

We ask God a question or questions, creating space and time in our lives to hear from Him (Step One).

We do background research taking our question(s) and researching what the Word of God, the Bible, says about the topic (Step Two).

Listening for His voice and researching the Word of God should lead us to a hypothesis of what we believe God is speaking to us (Step Three).

We share what we believe God is speaking to us with trusted friends or counselors—testing to see if they confirm what we are hearing (Step Four).

We analyze what we have heard through His voice, His Word, His counsel through others, and see if our conclusion is confirmed by His peace (Step Five).

Finally, we tell others of what we have learned through this process and of what God has done in our lives (Step Six).

THE EXPERIMENT

God invites each one of us to know His thoughts. Amos 3:7 says, "Surely the Lord God does nothing, unless He reveals His secret to His servants"[2] God wants to reveal His secrets to us, but we must seek Him. So, as you read through the chapters of this book, I invite you to participate in an experiment. A scientific supernatural experiment of sorts, which I am confident will help you grow exponentially in being able to hear and discern God's voice.

My challenge to you is to spend thirty minutes a day with God for forty days, intentionally positioning yourself to hear from Him. Thirty minutes is a good starting point, and I believe that as you begin to encounter God in prayer and His Word, your thirty minutes will soon turn into forty minutes or more. Thirty minutes a day of prayer, study and allowing God's Word to bring transformation can lead to a radically changed life.

There is detailed guidance on how to position yourself to hear from God in Part Three of this book (The Experiment—Guide to Hearing God's Voice). To help you effectively spend your thirty minutes with God and increase your receptivity to hear from— make contact with—Him, I unpack the five-step process I recommend for your devotional time:

Step One: Pick a Time and a Place to Meet with God

Step Two: Be Still and Worship

Step Three: Read and Pray

Step Four: Listen and Write

Step Five: Share and Obey

The Experiment—40 Days of Hearing God's Voice Workbook includes forty daily Bible passages to study, a format to follow to help you in your time with Him, and space to journal and record what you are learning and hearing.

The theologian Frank Laubach stated, "Before a scientist tries an experiment, he must have faith in the work of those who already have reported success."[3] This book is a combination of what I have learned from walking with God and listening to Him and gleaning from the wisdom and experience of others who have gone before me.

I believe that this book could change your life, but it won't happen without an intentional investment on your part. Will you say "yes" and commit to the experiment of spending thirty minutes for forty days seeking Him? As you take this step toward God and position yourself to hear from Him, He will come. Just as He said to the Israelites in Exodus 29:42, "I will meet with you and speak with you."[4] Get ready!

THE SCIENCE-LOVING, WANT-TO-BE INVENTOR

As a child, I was one of those quintessential science-loving, want-to-be inventors that wanted to compete in every science fair and had a certain obsession with creating something I could patent. My dream vacation was a trip to the Smithsonian Air and Space and Natural Science Museum in Washington D.C. It was there that I felt like I found *my people*, and realized I was not alone in my passion to discover.

That trip was a catalyst that pushed me further into my desire to explore and discover. If I was going to be the next Einstein or Edison, I figured I better start learning to split atoms and to create something that would revolutionize society. Okay, maybe not splitting atoms, but I felt inspired to dive head first into the world of science.

During those elementary years, it probably did not help my social status that I spent my free time reading science books and dreaming up what my next invention would be. I don't like to brag, but I will tell you that I entered six different science fairs and came home with more than my fair share of prizes. In fact, one year I won first prize in the school and an honorable mention in the regionals.

As a junior "mad scientist," I had one experiment go wrong...*very wrong*. It all started innocently enough on Christmas morning of my sixth grade year when I received the best present EVER. To me, it was the magnum opus of all Christmas gifts: my very own genuine chemistry set. Other boys my age were asking for autographed footballs, a new leather bomber jacket, or cassette tapes of Guns 'n Roses, but who would want such frivolous items when you could have beakers and potent chemicals—nitrates and sulfates—to mix together?

Upon receipt of the gift, I rushed upstairs to my room that was perfectly sequestered from the rest of house to mix up some concoctions without any interruptions from my parents. The chemistry set came with a plethora of different chemicals, different sized beakers, and an instruction book.

As I was the type of kid that never did anything by the book, I think it is fair to say that the instruction manual was probably never even opened. I mean who needs instruction manuals when you have chemicals, beakers, and a mad scientist mind?

In the confines of my private laboratory (aka my bathroom), I began to mix different chemicals together. Each time I watched with awe and excitement wondering what would happen next. Sometimes the different concoctions would voraciously bubble out of the beaker and other times they would change colors right before my eyes, but nothing had prepared me for the concoction that accidentally turned my beaker into a flying rocket.

I am still not quite sure what I mixed together or why it turned suddenly explosive. All I remember is pouring the last chemical in and the beaker shooting out of my hand and hitting the ceiling. To my horror, I noticed a burning smell and an atrocious discolored stain on the ceiling. I somehow managed to avoid ever telling my parents (if you are reading this Mom and Dad, I'm sorry...please forgive me). Sometime later, after we had moved out of that house, it burned down. I couldn't help wondering if there was a connection to the chemicals on the ceiling from my science experiment gone awry.

Obviously I can't say all my "experiments" were successful, but my obsession with science, and discovering why and how things in the natural world worked continued for the rest of my middle school years. I was a committed explorer of things in the natural until I had my first encounter with the supernatural on what was to be my, well, my death-bed.

THE VISION, THE WORD AND THE HEALING

I will never forget the day I was diagnosed with terminal cancer. As a fifteen-year-old given only six weeks to live, I was petrified, confused, and in disbelief all at the same time. It was a game-changer moment in my life.

The first sign of sickness came during a tennis match at age fourteen. All of a sudden in the middle of the match, I doubled over in pain and began regurgitating a water-like substance. I visited a myriad of doctors over the next year who tried to find a diagnosis for the painful symptoms I was experiencing. The doctors were baffled as to the cause, but the frequency of the incidents continued to increase until they were happening daily, even sometimes hourly, by the time I turned fifteen.

By this point, I had dropped in weight from 165 lbs. to 110 lbs., and although we did not know what was wrong with me, we knew it was serious. At the age when most boys are thinking about school dances, sports, and learning to drive, I entered The Ochsner Clinic in New Orleans for two weeks of intense tests and examination by a panel of at least twenty different doctors.

After a series of tests including a liver biopsy, a bone marrow test, and a spinal tap, I was diagnosed with a form of Leukemia called Eosinophilia, a condition that develops when the bone marrow makes too many eosinophils (a type of white blood cell). The doctors said there was nothing that they could do and planned to send me home with a life expectancy of six weeks. The day before I was supposed to leave the hospital the doctors took one more bone marrow test and a spinal tap, as I lay in the hospital bed in a state of devastation and disbelief over the prognosis I had received.

Sometime during that day, my grandfather, who had been like a second father to me, called the hospital to speak with me. My grandfather was a man whom I deeply respected and loved. As a young boy I spent countless hours with him, visiting his house almost every day where he helped me with my science experiments and building projects and spoke into my life as a mentor.

In his call, Grandfather told me about a vision that the Lord had given him where he saw me going up to heaven sickly in a hospital bed and then coming back down from the clouds healthy and dressed in normal clothes. My grandfather spoke with a humble confidence, "You are going to be healed. The Lord told me in prayer."

Although I was not walking with the Lord yet, I immediately clung to those words. My grandfather's words had weight in my life and what he spoke to me over the phone that afternoon became a source of hope in one of the darkest hours in my life.

Not long after my grandfather shared the vision, lying there alone in my hospital bed, I realized that my previous symptoms had dissipated. The vomiting that had occurred like clockwork almost every fifteen minutes had stopped, and the physical weariness that had hung over me like a wet blanket had lifted. I knew the tests would come back clear, but I was still in awe when the doctors came in the room to give me the results of what was to be the last tests before I was released to return home to die.

The doctor said, "We can't explain this, but...." He continued, "...there is nothing wrong with you." It was a classic response from a medical professional encountering a supernatural healing without basis in science or medicine. Every trace of Leukemia had miraculously vanished from my body! I left the hospital that day 100 percent healthy knowing that the One True God had healed me.

The Apostle Paul reminds us in 1 Corinthians 4:20 that the "kingdom of God is not a matter of talk but of power." My healing was undeniable evidence of the supernatural realm invading the natural. This was my first encounter with the supernatural. I not only experienced complete healing, but I knew beyond a shadow of a doubt that my grandfather heard a personal message from God. Although it was a few years later before I surrendered my life to God, after that day in the hospital I was marked. I had encountered God and the supernatural realm, and I wanted more.

After I gave my life to God in college, my previous quest to explore science and the natural world became an insatiable search to encounter God and experience more of the supernatural.

EXPLORING THE SUPERNATURAL

Scientists are devoting their lives to explore the depths of the natural realm, but who is giving their life to explore the depths of the supernatural? The current proposed budget for the US government to spend on scientific research and development is $143 billion dollars a year. That is just a fraction of what universities and businesses in the private sector spend researching science and the natural world. We often prioritize exploring the natural world, which is a valid search, but I think there is a greater search.

The man whose name has become synonymous with science concurs. Albert Einstein once said, "I want to know how God created this world. I am not interested in this or that phenomenon, in the spectrum of this or that element. I want to know His thoughts; the rest are details."[5] Although unfortunately, Einstein never professed personal faith in God, he said God's thoughts are what he wanted to know more than anything else.

When I was younger I wanted to be like Einstein because of the incredible advances he made in discovering aspects of the natural world, but now I want to be like Einstein because he realized all the scientific discoveries in the world paled in comparison to exploring the supernatural realm of knowing God's thoughts.

PART TWO

THE PRACTICAL SCIENCE OF HEARING GOD'S VOICE

"The best scientists and explorers have the attributes of kids! They ask questions and have a sense of wonder. They have curiosity. 'Who, what, where, why, when, and how!' They never stop asking questions, and I never stop asking questions, just like a five year old."[6]

Sylvia Earle—Marine Biologist, Explorer, Author and Lecturer

"The art and science of asking questions is the source of all knowledge."[7]

Thomas Berger—American Novelist

"If any of you lacks wisdom, you should ask God, who gives generously to all without finding fault, and it will be given to you." (James 1:5)

T he first step in the scientific method is asking a question about something that is observed. The question can be a *How, What, When, Who, Which, Why* or *Where* type question. It all boils down to what the scientist wants to learn. If the scientist wants to understand the cosmos better, he or she might ask, "Which planets rotate around the sun?" or "How are the planets affected by space debris?"

Do you remember your early years in elementary school planting a bean seed in a disposable cup? You probably didn't realize it at the time, but that was science, and you were being taught the first steps in the scientific method. The questions you might have asked include, "How do plants grow?" "What happens to a seed when it is stuck deep in dark soil, moistened by water and warmed by the sun?" As part of your experiment your teacher probably presented some research on the topic, and you hypothesized that based on the effects of the soil, water and sun your little bean seed would eventually sprout and become a bean plant.

In *Contact: The Practical Science of Hearing from God*, the first step begins with a question(s) for God. As a believer I know, that as Creator and Lord of the universe, He has all wisdom and certainly has the answers to my questions. Questions similar to those listed above: "*What* is His will for me in my family, work, ministry or career?" "*Where* does He want me to live?" "*Which* house should I purchase?" "*Why* is life so difficult during this season?" or "*How* should I speak to my child about his disobedience?"

As God, He desires to have a relationship with us where we have open communication: expressing our heart and desire and questions to Him, and He expressing His heart and desires back to us, and answering our questions with His wisdom and direction. I want that kind of relationship with God, and I'm sure you do too. The question part is easy; everybody has questions for God. However, hearing the answers from God often seems to elude us. So, how does God answer our questions?

HE CLEARS HIS THROAT

I know I'm not the only one who has wished that God would speak with an audible voice or at least give an occasional message written in the sky when seeking Him for direction. Many times, soon after giving my life to Jesus, I remember thinking, *God, I want to follow you and choose what you want me to choose. Why can't you just drop a blueprint from heaven? That would make this so much easier.*

God does not typically speak in an audible voice, and I have yet to receive a blueprint from heaven. However, I have found that He is true to His promise spoken through the prophet Jeremiah, "You will seek me and find me when you seek me with all your heart" (Jer. 29:13). It is important to note that God does not promise to be found by those that seek Him half-heartedly; but if our hearts are intent on seeking Him and obeying Him, we will find Him. The truth is: God wants to be found by those who really want to find Him.

I think about this truth when I play hide-and-go-seek with my boys. I can typically find where they are hiding in a matter of moments because I hear them giggling, wrestling around, or see their little feet hanging halfway out from under the bed. I think their favorite part of the game is when I find them. They hide in order to be found. I believe the same can be said of God. Meister Eckhart, a thirteenth-century German theologian, expressed this spiritual truth my boys taught me about the delight of being found, "God is like a person who clears His throat when hiding and so gives Himself away."[8]

The Old Testament prophet Isaiah said it like this, "Truly you are a God who has been hiding Himself, the God and Savior of Israel" (Isa. 45:15). Why does God remain hidden to a degree? Why does He not always speak to us in the overt ways we would so prefer? I believe He is looking for those who will look for Him.

Proverbs 25:2 says, "It is the glory of God to conceal a matter; to search out a matter is the glory of kings." God loves it when we search Him out. He is inviting each one of us on a divine game of hide-and-go-seek, during which He clears His throat so that those who are listening can easily find Him. He wants to teach each of us how to discern His voice and promptings.

The longer you walk with Him and the more you value His voice in your life, the easier it is to discern. Hearing His voice has been compared to a radio picking up airwaves. Radio waves are constantly floating through the air, but you need a radio receiver to pick up the sounds. Like the radio waves, God is always speaking; we just have to learn to tune our frequency to hear what He is saying. Jesus explains in John 10 that hearing from God is meant to be a reality in every believer's life.

I know some churches teach that we can't hear His voice today. They teach that God only speaks through what is written in His Word: The Bible. God certainly speaks to us through His Word. The whole next chapter focuses on the ways that God speaks through the Bible, and that nothing He speaks will ever contradict His written Word. However, the written Word is certainly not the only way He speaks.

Logos vs. *Rhema*

There are two Greek New Testament terms, that pastors often reference, that are translated as <u>word</u> in the New Testament: *logos* and *rhema*. The first word, *logos*, refers to the written Word of God—the Bible—and also to the living Word, Jesus (see examples in Luke 8:11, John 1:1, Philippians 2:16). The second term, *rhema*, means an utterance or spoken word (found in Luke 1:38; 3:2; 5:5 and Acts 11:16).

For you and me, a *rhema* is the Holy Spirit speaking to us in the present moment, through thoughts, ideas, dreams, visions, and inner knowing or warning, and through the words of others: i.e. a preacher, counselor, friend or even a total stranger. God's *rhema* word to us will usually deal with specific current circumstances, and may give us direction, warning or confirmation about something God wants us to do. However a *rhema* word will never contradict God's written Word—the Bible—the *logos*. In other words, God will never tell you to do something that is against principles in the Bible.

As you follow the steps outlined in this book, you will see that I encourage you as you hear from God that you submit what you believe God is saying to you to the written Word (*logos*) and also share it with a trusted, spiritually mature friend. If God is really speaking to you, His words will stand up to the test and be confirmed by His written Word and His counsel through others.

LISTENING FOR THE VOICE

"The one who enters by the gate is the Shepherd of the sheep. The gatekeeper opens the gate for Him, and the sheep listen to His voice. He calls His own sheep by name and leads them out. When He has brought out all his own, He goes on ahead of them, and his sheep follow Him because they know His voice. But they will never follow a stranger; in fact, they will run away from him because they do not recognize a stranger's voice." (John 10:2-5)

This passage teaches us that we have an active role to play in listening to His voice. In it, John explains that we follow Him because we know His voice and that we will not follow a stranger's voice.

I love that God speaks to us through metaphors so that we can understand spiritual truth through natural symbolism. One of the interesting facts I learned when I was studying about sheep is that they really do learn the voice of their particular shepherd. If there are a thousand sheep all together in a pasture and five hundred of the sheep belong to one shepherd, only five hundred sheep will respond to his call. The other five hundred will stay in the pasture because to them it is a stranger's voice calling, and they have learned not to respond.

John 10:27 reiterates this same principle, "My sheep listen to my voice; I know them, and they follow me." Notice the passage does not say "my super spiritual sheep" or "my full-time ministry sheep" will know my voice. It simply says my sheep will know my voice. This is a promise for all believers.

We learn to quickly recognize the voice of the ones that we love and those whose voices have weight in our lives. I remember when my wife, Taryn, and I were dating in the days before cell phones and caller ID; I could recognize it was her voice as soon as the first word was out of her mouth. After thirteen years of marriage, her voice has become even more familiar to me. Let's say she calls and says, "Hey babe!" and I say, "Who is this?" If she replies, "It's me" and I say, "Me who?" I don't have to be a prophet to know that I am going to be sleeping on the sofa that night.

Although I can't always recognize God's voice with the same clarity or certainty that I can recognize Taryn's, I have placed focus and effort into discerning and obeying His voice because I love Him and His words have weight in my life.

Discerning His Voice

How can we know we are hearing the voice of God, versus the voice of the enemy or the voice of our personal desires? Ask yourself the following questions:

- Is what I am hearing unclear or confusing?
- Does what I hear contradict the Bible?
- If I act on what I am hearing, will it lead me into compromise?

The voice of the enemy is often unclear and confusing, frequently contradicts Bible truths and ultimately leads you into sin and compromise. In the Garden of Eden, the

Discerning His Voice (cont.)

serpent deceived Eve by adding to, omitting, twisting and questioning what God said.

The confusion in his words contradicted the simple directions that God had given Adam, and eventually led Adam and Eve into sin.

Satan did the same when he tempted Jesus in the wilderness. He quoted Scripture to Jesus, but the motive was to tempt Jesus towards selfishness and disobedience to the call of God.

It was pulling on the human desires that Jesus likely had for food and authority, but offering such outside of the will of God.

The key to discerning between God and the enemy's voice and our own comes by familiarity through practice. The longer you walk with God the easier it becomes to distinguish between the three. It is often easiest to discern between God's voice and the enemy's voice; it is more difficult to discern between your human voice and God's.

Don't let not knowing whether an idea is from you or God paralyze you. If it seems like it is something that would be pleasing to God and agrees with His character and Word, take a step toward it as you remain in dialogue with the Lord asking Him to redirect you if it is not the best path for you.

God looks at the intention of the heart and if it is to please Him; you can trust he will not let you miss anything.

Discerning His Voice (cont.)

Based on the three questions I asked above, if what you are hearing is unclear or confusing, wait until the direction is clear. If what you are hearing contradicts the Bible in any way, even if it seems clear, do not act on it. If what you are hearing will lead you into sin in your actions, attitude or speech, it is not God.

God is not a God of confusion, but peace (see I Corinthians 14:33), God will never contradict His Word, and if He is speaking to you and leading you by His Spirit, He will never direct you into gratifying the desires of your flesh (see Galatians 5:16). Isaiah 30:21 says, "Whether you turn to the right or to the left, your ears will hear a voice behind you, saying, 'This is the way; walk in it.'" I have found that this voice brings joy, clarity, and further revelation, and even when I am not 100 percent sure of the origin of a thought, I can trust that as I continue to seek Him, He will guide me in the way I should walk, just as this verse promises.

There is a great story in 1 Kings Chapter 19. The great prophet Elijah had just come through a season of powerful ministry—was physically, emotionally and spiritually exhausted—and was running in fear after being threatened by his enemy, Jezebel. In his exhaustion, Elijah's perspective becomes one of self-pity, but the Lord continues to minister to him, feeding him and providing water, and allowing him to sleep. God's desire is to restore his servant so he can continue with the call and purpose that God has for his life.

In 1 Kings 19:11 Elijah is hiding in a cave and God tells him to stand outside on the mountain because He is going to pass by. Three dramatic signs happen. First there is a wind that tore apart the mountain, but the Lord was not in the wind. Second there was a great earthquake, but the Lord was not in the earthquake. Third there was a fire, but the Lord was not in the fire. After the fire there was a "still, small voice."

Although the wind, earthquake and fire were probably a dramatic response of the creation to the presence of the Lord, Elijah did not respond to any of these signs. It was when he heard the still, small voice of the Lord that the Bible says he put his cloak over his face and stood at the mouth of the cave to hear what God wanted to say. As Elijah responded to the still, small voice, he received his next set of directions.

As you learn to attune your ears to hear the still, small voice of the Lord, there are a few things that can be produced or evidenced by that voice, so I encourage you to look for the following these six occurrences:

1. **Strong Recurring Thought:** One of the most common ways I hear His voice is through a recurring thought or idea. As explained earlier, this is often a *rhema* word from God that comes through <u>our</u> thoughts. I have learned to pay close attention to my thoughts, especially recurring ones, and ask God if these are ideas from Him.

2. **An Idea with Genuine Excitement:** Generally when God is calling you to do something there is an excitement about

that area. There are times where He is calling you to do something difficult and there is not a natural excitement, but it is typically superseded by the excitement of knowing that He is calling you and will be with you.

3. **Deep, Calming Peace:** Colossians 3:15 explains that God's peace is a gift He gives us to help guide us. It is a supernatural confirmation of His presence with us and a way He confirms where He is leading. We will explore this topic more thoroughly in chapter four.

4. **An Inner Warning, Caution or "Check":** God in His kindness allows us to discern that certain decisions are not the wisest or best. It is up to us to heed these warnings and choose to go a different path when we sense an inner check or caution.

5. **A Supernatural Knowing:** When you have a strong inclination about something that feels certain and is too deep to be a natural understanding. This is more than intuition, as it is a supernatural understanding from the Lord. However, because of the subjective nature of our inclinations, we must test it, just as we test the other ways we hear from God.

6. **Open Doors:** Revelation 3:7 says that God will open doors that no man can shut and shut doors no man can open. We will explore this idea further in this chapter, but I encourage you to be looking for open doors of opportunity and to ask God if He is leading you through those doors.

Obviously not every door that opens before you is God leading you in that direction, but I have learned to look for open doors as a way that God speaks and leads.

THE SEEDS OF VISION

He subtly speaks to me every day through His still, small voice, and little nudges and ideas that I know did not come from me or even through my desires. However, there have also been monumental times that God has spoken to me that I would place in the *game changer* category. I have documented each of these milestone moments in the back of my Bible with their corresponding date. One of the most significant game changer moments came on April 22, 2005.

I was at a retreat center in the Shenandoah Valley for a doctoral course. Our professor, Dr. Mara Crabtree, taught the class about stewarding the dreams that God had placed in our heart. She shared a passage in Genesis explaining that there were many years between the time when Joseph first received the dream God had for his life and the time that the dream was fulfilled. She then gave us a handful of seeds that were supposed to represent the dreams that God had placed in our hearts. Planting the seeds was meant to be symbolic of the season of stewarding our dreams before they came to fruition. With the rest of the class, I planted my seeds outside the chapel at the retreat center. I knew that my seeds represented the church that Taryn and I had long felt called to plant in the Washington D.C. area.

Planting a church had been a dream in my heart since 1998, but the dream felt vague and seemed way too big for me. (This is actually a great litmus test to show that it is a God-sized dream. He doesn't want to give us a dream that we can accomplish in our strength or own talents because He wants to show us that He can do immeasurably more through us than we could ask or even imagine.)

I had actually shared this dream with Taryn on our first date. Some guys may stick to the light stuff on the first date like asking about the girl's favorite food or where she grew up, but evidently not me. I knew there was a call on both of our lives to do something great for God, and I began to pursue her to see if we were meant to walk together in the dream of planting a church in D.C. After I felt God's "yes," I asked her to marry me the spring of 2002 (after a few course corrections, which I will share with you more about in chapter four). We were married that summer, and we both knew we were called to plant a life-giving, multicultural church in the Washington D.C. area. What we didn't know was when or how it would happen.

After I planted the seeds my professor had given me, I looked down at the formation in which the seeds were planted—I noticed there were seventeen seeds planted in a circle and three up above it to the side. At that moment, I sensed the Holy Spirit whisper, "You will plant seventeen churches in the D.C. Metro area (the seventeen seeds represented the seventeen campuses we would plant around the D.C. area) and three up in New York (represented by the three seeds off to the side)." This was one of the clearest voices I have heard in my life, and I know that I know it was the Living God speaking to me. For the next two years, Taryn and I continued to seek God and wait on His timing for how and when we should launch the church.

LOOK EXPECTANTLY

The Hebrew word for <u>wait</u> is *qavah* meaning to "look expectantly." The definition demonstrates that waiting on the Lord is not a passive activity. Rather, it is actively seeking where He is moving, so we are ready to step forward when it is time.

Waiting on the Lord has been a significant theme in DC Metro Church's story. The spring before DC Metro launched in 2007, two of my closest friends from graduate school who would help me plant the church, Matt Stroia and Julie Reams, and I visited the D.C. area to fast, pray, and walk the streets asking God to open up the location He had for what would become DC Metro Church. We investigated over twenty-five locations, knocked on countless doors, and even sent chocolates and flowers to one of the school superintendents hoping to gain relational favor and possibly an opportunity to use one of the area schools. All twenty-five-plus doors were closed—very humbling!

One day, Matt was laying in his bed thinking about the future church when a Middle Eastern restaurant he had visited in Alexandria popped into his mind. He was puzzled as to why he was thinking about food. He was about to attribute it to random, wandering thoughts or hunger, when he decided to ask God if this thought was somehow connected to the church. He immediately thought about the movie theater, the Regal Potomac Yard Theater, down the street from the restaurant. Was this God's voice speaking through a picture in his mind's eye?

Thoughts and Ideas

Just like Matt experienced the thought of the Middle Eastern restaurant popping into his head, God will sometimes speak to us through thoughts, ideas or a picture in our imagination. In February 2014, I experienced God speaking to me through a recurring thought. DC Metro Church was close to making an offer on a large church facility in Maryland that was in foreclosure (The building was the size of one-and-a-half Super Walmart stores).

Our board had signed off on making an offer, and although I still didn't have complete peace about it, we were moving forward with an offer that we expected would be accepted.

A short time before the offer was to be made I was sitting in a local pastor's gathering called City Fathers. Pastor Mark Batterson, who was leading the gathering, said he believed God was going to speak to each of us that day about our area of greatest need. As I bowed my head, and was thinking about that potential property, a thought came to my mind: *Take Virginia First!* It was a thought that I heard over and over again that day at the gathering and many times over the following weeks. For me and the church it was God's direction to not purchase the property in Maryland, but focus future expansion in Virginia—something that is happening as I write.

Another time I experienced Him speaking to me through a great idea. I was on my way home to spend a date night with my wife. The church was in the middle of a fast from food and media, so I couldn't take her to a restaurant or to a movie. I wanted to have a special date night with my wife,

Thoughts and Ideas (cont.)

and I asked the Lord if He had any ideas of what we could do together. I had a thought that was too good to be mine: take Taryn to all the houses God had provided for us to live in during our time in D.C., and other places significant to what He had done through DC Metro Church. As we stopped in front of each location, we took time to pray a prayer of thanks for God's blessings. The God-inspired idea was both spiritual and romantic!

God can speak to us through thoughts and ideas and also through pictures in our imaginations where instead of words or thoughts we see an image. Similar to the other ways that God speaks to us, submit thoughts, ideas and images to the written Word, the Bible, and when necessary to godly counsel. The source of our thoughts can be God, self or even the enemy, so it is important to test them. Remember nothing from God will contradict the Bible. If you are unclear of the source or interpretation of a thought, it can be tested and weighed with the help of some spiritually mature friends.

The absolute incredible part of the story is that while Matt was having this interaction with God, God was speaking to me too about the movie theater. I had just heard about a church in Florida that had started in a movie theater, so I began to research theaters in the Alexandria area. I had the Regal movie theater site still open on my computer when Matt called me that afternoon to ask me my thoughts on starting the church in the Potomac Yard Theater. Talk about incredible confirmation that this was the location we were to pursue! Needless to say, I immediately contacted the theater to see if they would be open to a church meeting in one of the theaters. After a ton of discouraging closed doors, this door essentially flew open...and the rest, as they say, is history. The moment we secured the theater, I was overwhelmingly thankful for all the closed doors knowing that all twenty-five plus facilities that rejected us paled in comparison to the theater.

We had a similar journey while searching for our first campus location. Because the Lord had so clearly spoken to me in 2005 that the church would have seventeen campuses throughout the D.C. area and three in the New York area, becoming a multi-site church had been in our hearts from the beginning. What the Lord did not tell me was when or how. During the third year of the church, we began seeking God to see if it was time to start the first campus. Over the next two years, we sought out over thirty potential campus locations. Similar to our search five years earlier, we encountered closed door after closed door...until—you guessed it—another Regal movie theater, this time in Fairfax, Virginia.

Throughout the process we had been praying the prayer from Revelation 3:7, for open doors that no man can shut. The Fairfax area was already on the radar of our leadership team as a strategic area to start our first campus, so we were thrilled when this location opened up. We saw God's fingerprints in this choice, as our first sanctuary was a Regal movie theater in Potomac Yard. Somehow it seemed right in step that the door that God chose to open for our first campus would bring us back to our roots in a Regal theater. Thus, we officially became one church in two locations on January 13, 2013 with the launching of our Fairfax campus.

WHEN GOD SAYS "NO!"

The number of closed doors we experienced before we initially launched the church and before we launched the first campus illustrates an important principle we find in the Apostle Paul's life. God often speaks through a "no" before He says "yes" to what is actually the very best choice for us. I am not always the biggest fan of hearing God say "no" because I am so ready for Him to say "yes," but I have seen time and time again how the "no" is actually a gift as He is at work to bring into alignment His best and highest for me.

Modern day "theologian" Garth Brooks had this same revelation in his song "Unanswered Prayer" which hit #1 on the Country Billboards in the '90s. Brooks talks about taking his wife to a hometown football game and running into his girlfriend from high school. As he introduced the two women, he began to remember how much he had desired his girlfriend back in the day, praying each night that if God would give her to him for all time, he would never ask for anything again.

Although he doesn't tell us what had happened to the old girlfriend over the years, Brooks ends the song thanking God for unanswered prayers; that God still cares even if He doesn't answer prayers—and actually some of His greatest gifts are those unanswered prayers. I think all of us in hindsight can thank God for some unanswered prayers in our lives. As author Tim Keller says, "God will only give you what you would have asked for if you knew everything He knows."9

We see this same principle of God saying "no" before He says "yes" to direct the Apostle Paul where to go in Acts 16. The Apostle Paul is my favorite to learn from about hearing God's voice because he did not walk with Jesus while Jesus was on the earth. The other apostles had the advantage of hearing His voice before His ascension, but Paul had his first encounter with the ascended Jesus on the road to Damascus in Acts 9. Like you and I, he had to learn to discern the promptings and leadings of the Holy Spirit. From the start of Paul's ministry in Acts 9 until Acts 16, we see that he received very distinct direction on where to go and what to do, but it does not clearly explain how he discerned where to go until Acts 16. In fact, I believe Acts 16 reveals his grid for how you and I can discern His voice.

In Acts 16:6-10, there is a process that Paul is taken through that gives much insight on how to discern the guidance of the Holy Spirit for our own lives.

> They passed through the Phrygian and Galatian region, having been forbidden by the Holy Spirit to speak the word in Asia; and after they came to Mysia they were trying to go into Bithynia and the Spirit of Jesus did not permit them; and passing by Mysia, they came down to Troas. A vision appeared to Paul in the night, a man of Macedonia was standing and appealing to him and saying, "Come over to Macedonia and help us." When he had seen the vision, immediately we sought to go into Macedonia concluding that God had called us to preach the gospel to them.

In Acts 16:6 we see Paul learning where he is *not* to go. It seems to reveal that if there is a place that we specifically should not go, then we can infer that there is a place that we *are* to go. It is significant to observe that the passage says that the Spirit of Jesus would not *let* them go. I don't know about you, but I had to learn the hard way that it is not worth it if God does not want me to go somewhere. Now, when I feel a hesitation in my spirit or a check from the Lord about a certain direction, I have learned to more quickly say, "I'm not going."

The next thing that we observe from the text is that Paul comes to the end of the road in Troas. It seems highly probable that Paul came to a point here where he started to doubt. He had just tried to go two other places and they were both obviously blocked by the hand of God—let's call them closed doors. Perhaps he thought that God was going to block everywhere and anywhere he wanted to go.

This is helpful to remember when we are having trouble discerning the will of God. Even Paul, the man God used to change the course of history in the Roman world, could not always immediately discern God's direction. I've learned in order to enjoy the process with God I have to focus on the outcome or reward. It's similar to eating a Cadbury Egg. You have to unwrap it to get to something better than you could even imagine. God seems to delight in the relationship and trust that is formed when we have to continue to look to Him for each step of the journey.

I like to call this *progressive revelation* where He gives us just what we need to know when we need to know it. I naturally prefer to know where the path is going to lead before I start my journey, but God kindly reminds me that He is walking with me. He invites me to enjoy the adventures we will go on together and promises to help me navigate every twist and turn along the way—and at the end of the day that is all I need to know.

In verse nine, we see that in the night, in what may have been Paul's moment of despair, a vision came to him. All Scripture tells us is that it came to him "in the night." It is not stated whether he was sleeping and he woke up or if he was walking along the road and the vision came to him as he walked. However, the most important thing is the content of his vision. He had a vision of a man that needed his help in Macedonia.

Dreams and Visions

Two additional ways God will speak to us is through dreams and visions. There is a prophetic word that appears in the Old Testament book of Joel and later in Acts 2:17. The word talks about God pouring out His Spirit on all mankind in the last days. One of the results of this outpouring will be that "Your old men will dream dreams, your young men will see visions" (Joel 2:28).

The difference between a dream and a vision is that a dream takes place while you are asleep and a vision while you are awake.

In a dream God's Spirit often speaks to you through images. Sometimes the meaning of a God-inspired dream is very clear—a warning, or a sense of direction for something you had earlier asked God. Other times the meaning is not so clear—and will need some interpretation.

Dreams and Visions (cont.)

As a disclaimer, not all dreams are God-inspired. Our dreams can be influenced by different stimuli: random people and events strung together through subconscious thoughts, a mind that is racing with thoughts from your busy day; or even from the enemy. When in doubt if a dream is from God, or when you don't understand the meaning of a dream you believe is from Him—ask Him for wisdom to understand. James 5:1 affirms that God wants to give us wisdom if we ask.

A vision is like a spiritual movie playing in front of us or in our head while we are awake and conscious. Like a dream the vision may be clear in meaning, or may need some additional interpretation and understanding from God. If you do experience dreams or visions, submit them to the process that we are introducing in this book. See if the dream or vision's message is supported by the Bible (God will never contradict His written Word) and submit it to someone who is spiritually mature and whose counsel you trust.

Paul's night vision reveals something about the way God guides, but it also reveals something about Paul's heart. Paul was partnered with God. It seems to reveal that he sincerely wanted to go where he could help people. Why else would the Lord give him a vision of someone needing help? He did this because He knew that Paul wanted to go where he would be used to help people. Here we see God's sovereignty in choosing to guide Paul in a way that would relate to desires in his heart. Once we have submitted our hearts and lives to Christ, God often uses the desires of our heart to guide us into His will.

In verse nine, the Greek word *parakaleo* is translated into the English as "*appealing* to him" in reference to the man from Macedonia. This word means, "To call to, to beseech, and to exhort."[10] This brings us to a greater depth of understanding on what the passage is really stating. Further insight is gained by noting that the use of this word is "to call someone to oneself" not "to call to someone." It is evident from the Greek word chosen that this man in Macedonia needed help and that it did not matter where the help came from, it just mattered that the help came to him.

It is also significant to note that once Paul received guidance from the Lord, he was confident in putting that guidance into motion immediately. This word is derived from the Greek word *eutheos*, which means, "suddenly and straightway."[11] Thoralf Gilbrant explains in *The New Testament Greek-English Dictionary*, "Paul and his company did not hesitate once this positive guidance was given. They concluded that God had called them, therefore they acted."[12] As the old saying goes, "Slow obedience is no obedience." Paul's expedient obedience should be a model to all believers, that when we do receive guidance from the Lord, we are to act upon it quickly.

We can begin to see a pattern of guidance that the Lord used in Paul's life, especially concerning the geographic location of ministry. It is interesting to note that this discernment comes in two steps. First, God told Paul where *not* to go. Only after Paul was obedient to those instructions, God told him where he was to go.

This is not always the pattern, but as we discussed earlier, one of the ways that God often speaks is that He closes doors before He opens the right one. It is almost as if He is clarifying a single preferred path instead of multiple options.

God wants the type of relationship with us where we speak to Him and He speaks to us. His speaking to us can happen in many different ways: through His written Word—the Bible, a *rhema* word, thoughts and ideas, pictures and images, dreams and visions, an inner knowing or even through closed or open doors. As you have experienced God in step one of *The Practical Science of Hearing from God*, get ready to submit those questions you have asked God, or preliminary answers you think you have received to step two of the process: The Research.

CHAPTER TWO | THE RESEARCH

"Research is to see what everybody else has seen, and to think what nobody else has thought"[13]

Albert Szent-Gyorgyi—Hungarian Biochemist

"Somewhere, something incredible is waiting to be known."[14]

Dr. Carl Sagan—American Astronomer, Writer and Scientist

"Study to shew thyself approved unto God, a workman that needeth not to be ashamed, rightly dividing the word of truth." (2 Timothy 2:15)[15]

The second step in the scientific method is research. For the scientist this means using all the available tools: scientific journals, the internet, and other scientists, to gain the most information about how to answer the question being researched. Researching and collecting the most information before starting to experiment helps the scientist create his or her plan for answering their question, and make sure that they don't repeat mistakes from the past.

In *Contact: The Practical Science of Hearing from God*, the second step of research helps to either answer the question we asked in step one, or to confirm the answer we received from God to our question. As I mentioned in chapter one, I have asked God to speak to me in dramatic ways, and I love it when He does. However, I have found I often seek a spectacular sign from Him instead of spending time in Scripture—in research, "rightly dividing the word of truth" (2 Tim. 2:15)[16]—asking Him to speak to me through His Word.

HE SPEAKS THROUGH HIS WORD

God loves to reveal Himself to those that are seeking Him—doing research—through His Word. Jeremiah 29:13 says, "You will seek me and find me when you seek me with all your heart." In applying this verse, I have found that the more I seek him in His Word, the more He will speak.

When I was growing up, I had a distant respect for God's Word, but I also thought reading it was extremely boring and best suited for those in the retirement community. I viewed the Bible as a book with antiquated stories and as a manual on how to be good. Being good seemed quite dull, and I felt a certain cognitive dissonance whenever I heard someone read from the Bible. I went to church every Sunday, but I definitely did not love His Word.

In my high school and college years I drifted farther from Jesus. During my junior year in college, I decided to spend a semester in Utah, away from all my LSU fraternity brothers, in an attempt to get a fresh start. After a semester of searching for the meaning of life to no avail, taking a myriad of drugs, and essentially living my same hedonistic lifestyle, I reached a low point. My move was an attempt to escape, but change seemed elusive. I could not escape myself.

However, while waiting for my parents at the airport, a man handed me a little book—an orange Gideon Bible containing the

New Testament, Psalms, and Proverbs. My first thought was to tuck it away in my junk drawer, but my curiosity got the best of me. I opened to the book of Proverbs, and I could not put it down. Little did I know that the content in the little orange book would change the trajectory of my life. The wisdom and insight found in the verses of Proverbs seemed to leap off the page. How could this be the same book I had written off as obsolete and irrelevant?

This began my journey into reading through the New Testament and surrendering my life to this man named Jesus, who fascinated me. Over the years I can honestly say that I have fallen in love with the Bible. The more I love God's Word and revere it, digging into it and researching the truth between its covers, the more I recognize Him speaking to me. God invites all believers to truly love His Word and to hear Him speak to us with specific and personal clarity through His Word.

IT'S ALIVE!

One of my favorite passages is Hebrews 4:12 because it reminds us that God desires to speak to us and shape us through His Word, "For the Word of God is *alive* and active. Sharper than any double-edged sword, it penetrates even to dividing soul and spirit, joints and marrow; it judges the thoughts and attitudes of the heart." Do you know of any other book that claims to be alive?

The Holy Spirit helps God's Word come *alive* so that we can apply what we read to our lives. The Bible was written to be an invitation into an interactive conversation with God rather than just another book containing some wise sayings or principles. This means that although I can read the same passage again and again, the Holy Spirit will highlight new aspects each time or teach me how the passage applies to a particular circumstance. I love how specific and personal the Lord is.

For example, I was reading through Psalm 78 one morning before we moved my family across town into a new home. Taryn and I were already a little nervous for the kids and us, as it was a bit out of town— we were moving to "the country." While reading Psalm 78, I felt the Holy Spirit highlight verse 55, "He drove out nations before them and allotted their lands to them as an inheritance; he settled the tribes of Israel in their homes." A wave of peace came over me as I felt God speak a promise to me through His Word, "David, just as I settled the Israelites in their home, so I will settle you, Taryn, and your boys in your home."

That word from the Lord came at the perfect time. I have found that no matter how much we plan and prepare, moving is an unsettling ordeal. What encouraged me most was that I felt like He was saying that He would turn our house into a *home*—that He would truly settle us. I wrote "January 2012—Psalm 78:55" in the back of my Bible. I wanted to remember this promise from God and claim it as we transitioned. I can say now, this word truly came to pass as we made the move. The boys love our new place because of all the surrounding woods for them to explore, and it has become a respite to create memories together as a family. We feel truly settled.

Not long after our move, I was reading in Jeremiah 30 and verse two stood out to me, "This is what the Lord, the God of Israel, says: 'Write in a book all the words I have spoken to you.'" I've always dreamed of writing a book, but I needed some momentum and direction from God as to when to start. As I read this verse, I felt

God giving me the green light to begin writing. From this, I also realized His hand would be upon it as I recorded the words He had spoken to me. I wrote "April 2012—Jeremiah 30:2-3" in the back of my Bible because it was my word from the Lord to begin the book you are reading now.

CONFIRMATION THROUGH THE WORD

On the morning of June 15, 2010 I saw a vision—an animated picture in my mind's eye—during my time with God. In the vision I was standing on the bridge that is adjacent to our current church facility looking at our new building. I not only saw our current building but another large facility next door, as plain as day. Next I saw myself in the facility in what I understood to be a prayer tower that was several stories high overlooking Washington D.C. and the monuments. I was surrounded by my four kids who looked like they were teenagers and were praying with me for the city of D.C. I began to scribble the vision of what I saw on a nearby napkin. I sensed in my spirit that God was calling us to take steps towards acquiring the building and land next door to our facility, but I was not sure when or how it would happen.

We had just gone through an arduous year and a half process of acquiring permits and renovating our current facility to be able to move in just two months prior. It was a significant step in faith because our budget had to double to pay the bills in the new facility. I heard the still, small voice of God telling us to acquire that first facility, confirmed it with our Lead Team and Overseers (In chapter three we will talk about the importance of seeking counsel when you are making important decisions.) and stepped out in faith. God was completely true to His Word. In one month the budget of DC Metro doubled, which had not happened before and has not happened since. After that season of being stretched in the area of faith, the last thing on my mind was trying to acquire more property. I thought it might be time to have a relaxing, low-key summer, but evidently God had other plans.

During that time, I was studying the book of Joshua. The theme of the passages I was reading is the Israelites possessing the Promised Land. As I read, I felt Him stirring my heart through His Word about the call that He has on DC Metro to not only possess physical land, but to partner with Him in repossessing the land spiritually. There is a rich spiritual heritage upon which our country was founded, a godly foundation that our forefathers sought to implement. Unfortunately we have veered away from that foundation; but, God in His mercy is calling us to help restore a God-first culture throughout the D.C. Metro area.

In Joshua 6, Joshua leads the Israelites to march and pray around the city of Jericho as a prophetic declaration of the land they would possess. After reading Joshua and praying about the vision God gave me of the property next door, I felt led to go do my own Jericho march around the property. There was one significant obstacle: a gate around the property and a security guard in front of the building. I figured that if the Israelites could go boldly into Jericho to possess the Promised Land that was filled with giants and their enemies, then I could take down the security guard. I am only kidding!

As a pastor I decided it might be wise to try a different approach. I convinced Dana Sorensen, a staff member who has been a part of the church since the beginning, to go with me to try and convince the security guard to let us walk around the building. I was sure the guard was going to think we were crazy and was ready for her to turn us down, when to my surprise she said, "Sure, you can walk around the building, as long as I walk with you." The three of us began to circumnavigate the building. Pamela, the security guard, began to tell us her story. It happened to be her first night on the job and she shared how she was a believer who had recently returned to the Lord. When we were half way around the building she blurted out, "This may sound strange to you, but I feel like Rahab in the Bible who allowed Joshua and Caleb to spy out the land." Dana and I couldn't believe our ears. Did she just compare us to Joshua and Caleb? She had no idea that I had been studying the book of Joshua or that God had just given me a vision about possessing the land.

I believed in divine appointments before that night, but this further confirmed my belief that God absolutely is in the details of our life and that He strategically places certain people in our life for a specific purpose. As if that were not enough, God in His kindness wanted to bring me further confirmation. Two nights later on June 19th, we had the incredible privilege of Christine Caine coming to speak at our church. Chris Caine is one of the most passionate, dynamic preachers I know, who has acquired a reputation for speaking a prophetic word through the message she brings to a particular church. I felt especially excited about what Chris would preach that night. Believe it or not, her message was the story of Joshua and Caleb spying out the land from the same passage in Joshua I had been studying. At one point in the message, she pointed in the direction of the property next door and loudly proclaimed, "God is calling you to possess the land!" Dana and I were having trouble containing ourselves as we looked at each other with wide eyes and a knowing smile. God was confirming through His Word what He had earlier shown me in a vision.

Holy Txt Challenge

A few years after we planted DC Metro Church, God spoke to me to help the church learn what it means to fall in love with His Word. In a still, small voice I heard, "Read my Word." I realized that God was leading me to read His Word aloud to the church to awaken their hearts to His Word in a greater way. "Read my Word" was the game changer that inspired what I aptly called the Holy Txt Challenge.

The challenge was if one thousand people committed to reading the Word for twenty minutes a day for forty days, I would read the entire New Testament straight through in one consecutive reading. They unabashedly rose to the challenge. On Friday, May 11, 2012 at 7 p.m., the marathon began. I had an excitement in my heart and expectancy in my spirit because I know that something significant happens as we declare His powerful Word aloud.

The most exhilarating part of the challenge was reading the book of Revelation. The sanctuary was filled with a tangible faith and a palpable electricity, as so many DC Metroers joined us for the reading of the final book of the New Testament. On Saturday, May 12th a little after 5 p.m., I completed approximately twenty-two hours of reading 260 chapters, 7,956 verses and 138,020 words (and I consumed twenty cups of tea, twenty-four bottles of water, and three-

Holy Txt Challenge (cont.)

and-a-half bears of honey). My part of the Holy Txt Challenge was finished, but the catalytic effects were just beginning.

One DC Metroer shared, "During the Holy Txt Challenge, I felt the Word of God come alive for me like never before. My goodness! It was like all the cogs to an engine were coming into place in my head and heart as different pieces of the New Testament were being read, and then that engine started to turn, and revelation after revelation starting forming and gaining traction."

Another DC Metroer explained, "After hearing the reading of the whole New Testament, the Word became so much more approachable for me. I never realized that the whole book of Matthew could be read in approximately two hours. The Holy Txt Challenge created a desire for me to read and study the Bible more on my own, so that I can unlock the treasures in His Word."

Reflecting back to when God told me that He wanted DC Metroers to fall even more in love with His Word, I am encouraged to see how peoples' desire for the Word has increased. I am convinced that your love of His Word will grow too as you are faithful to read, study, and obey His Word. I encourage you to keep digging into your Bibles because He wants to reveal Himself to you. As A.W. Tozer said, "The Bible is not an end in itself, but a means to bring men to an intimate and satisfying knowledge of God, that they may enter into Him and delight in His Presence..."[17]

S-O-A-P

One of the most common questions I get as a pastor is how I study the Bible. What research methods do I use as I seek to answer my questions? My devotional times are very simple. I begin with a formula I learned years ago called S-O-A-P, created by Wayne Cordeiro, which is simply Scripture, Observation, Application, and Prayer.[18]

Scripture

The first step is simply to decide which passage you are going to study and then began reading it. In *The Experiment—40 Days of Hearing God's Voice Workbook* we helped you out by picking one Scripture passage for each of the forty days. After completing The Experiment, I recommend choosing a book of the Bible to read through, or doing a topical study with the help of a concordance. Some good books to start with are the Gospel of John, any of Paul's letters in the New Testament, or Psalms in the Old Testament. Proverbs is great as well as it has thirty-one chapters for a solid chapter a day for a month.

If you are interested in reading narratives about the lives of great men and women in the Bible, I recommend tracing the story of the patriarchs in Genesis, Moses and the Israelites' escape from Egypt in the book of Exodus, the adventures of King David in the books of 1 and 2 Samuel or Peter and Paul in the book of Acts.

If you prefer a topical study, you can go to a concordance and look up what you are interested in studying and it will lead you to passages and verses about that topic. Many study Bibles have concordances in the back or you can find incredible concordances online at locations such as biblestudytools.com.

For example, if I am studying about purpose, I would look up the word purpose and it would lead me to verses such as Psalm 138:7-8a, "Though I walk in the midst of trouble, you preserve my life; you stretch out your hand against the anger of my foes, with your right hand you save me. The Lord will fulfill [His *purpose*] for me." or Proverbs 19:21, "Many are the plans in a person's heart, but it is the Lord's *purpose* that prevails." I recommend choosing a chapter if you are studying a book or a few verses if you are doing a topical study. Once you have your chapter or verses selected, you are ready to move to the "O" or observation stage.

Observation

As you read Scripture, ask yourself, "What stands out?" Ask God, "What are you highlighting to me today?" For example, when I was studying the book of Joshua, the verse found in Joshua 1:8 stood out to me, "Keep this Book of the Law always on your lips; meditate on it day and night, so that you may be careful to do everything written in it. Then you will be prosperous and successful."

Here are some questions you can ask in the observation stage:

- What is the historical/contextual situation?

- When was it written?

- Who is speaking to whom?

- Why was it written?

- What kind of literary genre is it (Narrative, Command, Poetry, or Prophecy)?

- How does the author arrange the text? Look for repeated words or phrases and theological words (You can look these up if you do not know a definition or want to explore further).

- What does the passage say about God, Jesus, and the Holy Spirit?

- What does the passage say about the believer?

- What is the theme of the passage (the big idea)?

- What are the main principles you learn from this text (timeless truths)?

- What does the commentary or study Bible say about this passage and how does that add to your understanding?

A few observations I wrote about Joshua 1:8:

1. This passage is a command to "Keep this book of the law always."

2. There are three things we are commanded to do with the book of the law: speak about it ("on your lips"); continually think about it ("meditate on it day and night"); and, act on it ("do everything written in it").

3. The result of us fulfilling this command is biblical prosperity and success.

After you finish writing down some observations, you can move to the "A" or the Application step where you try to determine how the passage applies to those living in the 21st century and to your personal life.

Application

For the Application step, I made up my own acrostic called GOD SPA, which are intentional questions I ask to help apply the passage to my life. I want to not only read the Word, but I also want to let the Word read me. Besides, who doesn't like a little spa action?

Here are the six questions for you to ask:

1. **G (Growth)—Is there an area where God is calling you to grow?**

   Is there a part of God's Word that you know you are not walking in the fullness of what God has for you? Perhaps God is revealing something in your heart. Maybe He is highlighting a relationship or an area in your marriage that needs work. Perhaps it is in your finances, your health or something going on at work. Whichever area you feel Him revealing, I encourage you to surrender it to Him and ask Him to help you give Him full leadership.

2. <u>O</u> (Obedience)—Is there an area where God is calling you to obey?

Is there an area in your life that you are not obeying God right now? This can be similar and even overlapping with a growth area, but it is generally focused either on a specific action that you feel the Holy Spirit asking you to take or a particular command in His Word that you know you have not been following.

As I often tell my boys, delayed obedience is not really obedience. Like any good parent, God wants our wholehearted obedience, so we should honestly be asking the Holy Spirit if there is any area where we are not walking in full obedience. God will graciously meet us in that place to give us His strength to help us turn from these areas, as we are honest and authentic before Him.

3. <u>D</u> (Direction)—Is there a direction God is speaking to you through this passage?

We all desire God's perspective on what we should do next in life? One of my favorite verses on direction is Psalm 32:8, which says, "I will instruct you and teach you in the way you should go." I have found one of the most common ways that God gives me direction is through my time in the Word. When I have a decision coming up, I will draw away and pray and read to see if God highlights anything through Scripture. I find time and time again that the Word that has already been spoken by Him in His Word still speaks to me, just when I need it.

4. <u>S</u> (Sin)—Is there a sin God wants you to confess and turn from in this passage?

Sin sometimes sounds like a real religious word, but the Greek definition of sin is actually an archery term that means to "miss the mark." Often when I am reading the Word, God will bring to mind a certain area of my life, and I will realize that I haven't hit the mark for God's best for that area of my life.

If God points out an area in your life where you have missed the mark, you need to do two things: repent and confess. The Greek word for repentance, *metanoia*, means changing your mind about a former attitude or action. Recognizing that that attitude or action was wrong toward God or other people, and choosing to change your mind and turn away from it. Confession is a part of repentance. It is telling God you are sorry for missing the mark. The beauty is that I John 1:9 tells us "If we confess our sins, he is faithful and just and will forgive us our sins and purify us from all unrighteousness."

Conviction vs. Condemnation

I have found it extremely helpful to know the difference between conviction and condemnation. Conviction is when God points out sin in your life because He wants you to know that He has something better for you and that He will help empower you to choose His path. It is often an action that God wants you to take like, "Apologize to your worker for being selfish when you took the last sandwich at the luncheon without checking to see if he had eaten."

Condemnation is altogether different and from a different source. Condemnation is an attack from the enemy on your identity where he makes you feel guilty and weighed down. It is typically an accusation about who he says you are instead of a particular action you have done. For example, "You are a selfish person who is always looking out for yourself at the expense of others, and you'll never change."

As believers we need to know how to discern between conviction and condemnation. One of the best ways I have found to distinguish between these two is that conviction is life-giving and empowering. It is never easy to face up to the mistakes in our lives, but when God highlights an area where we have missed the mark, He does it because He loves us and will give us the power to change as we surrender it to Him.

5. **P (Promise)—Is there a promise from this passage you can claim for your life?**

Did you know that there are over 6000 promises in God's Word? For example, the passage Joshua 1:8 that we discussed earlier contains a clear promise. God promises that as I meditate and walk in the truths of His Word, He will make my way prosperous and successful. This is an example of a conditional promise, meaning God will fulfill His part on the condition that you fulfill your part.

We all would like to have some God success in our lives. In fact, the word prosper translates in Hebrew to mean "to be pushed forward in life." How about that as a promise for reading God's Word, that He will push you forward in life? God's Word is filled with promises that we can cling to and pray over ourselves when we are in a hard situation or when we need to be reminded of His truth.

6. **A (Accountability)—Is there any area where you need accountability?**

Accountability is a key to success, because whenever you come across one of the five application areas in your Bible study, there is probably an area where you're thinking to yourself, *you know what? I don't know if I'm going to be able to walk this out on my own. I know I've got God's help, but I think it would be wise to call someone to hold me accountable in this area.*

Many times, after spending time in the Word, I've picked up the phone to call one of my accountability partners. I have three men that I can call and say, "God is dealing with me, and I need you to regularly ask me about this area of my life."

By the way, no one can hold you accountable unless you tell that person where you're tempted. If they don't know where you're tempted, they're just going to ask you a general question like "Hey, how are you doing?" We are most likely to answer "fine." I'm fine because I don't want to talk to you about my real issues. Did you know that when we avoid accountability what we're actually saying is we don't really want to change?

I ask all six of these GOD SPA questions for the passage I am studying. Typically God will have me focus on a couple of these areas as He highlights how He wants me to apply a particular passage to my life.

For example, from Joshua 1:8, I felt led to focus on the Growth Area, Promise, and Accountability. I was challenged to increase my time in meditating on the Word (Growth Area) so that I can experience true success (Promise). I felt led to share this with a few close friends who will keep me accountable by asking me how this area is going which will encourage me to continue to intentionally study God's Word.

Prayer

In our S-O-A-P acrostic we've discussed Scripture, Observation, and Application. The final P in S-O-A-P is Prayer. Prayer is actually the most important step and one of the most forgotten. This is simply taking whatever God has spoken to you, the message that He has given to you and bringing it back to Him asking Him to help you. You might pray, "God I'm going to need some help with this. I'm going to try to walk this out today."

A great support for this step is two-way prayer journaling: you writing your thoughts to God and then writing what you believe God is speaking to you. King David was one of the toughest, fiercest warriors in Scripture, and he was a voracious journaler. A good portion of the book of Psalms is essentially David's journals crying out to the Lord and then listening and responding to what he hears. David received the plans for the temple his son Solomon would build in one of his times of journaling. In 1 Chronicles 28:19 David explains, "I have all of the plans in writing as a result of the Lord's hand on me, and He enabled me to understand all the details of the plan."

The prophet Habakkuk was no stranger to journaling. The first chapter of Habakkuk is essentially Habakkuk complaining to the Lord—which is a good reminder that we can be totally authentic with God when we are praying. He is asking God why it is taking Him so long to move in his situation. Before God answers him, He instructs Habakkuk to write down his answer. Habakkuk 2:2 says, "Write down the revelation and make it plain on tablets, so that whoever hears it may run with it."

In my first decade of walking with Him, I definitely did not love journaling. I watched Taryn pour her heart out in journal after journal during the years we were dating and the first years of marriage, but I just couldn't get into it. Several years ago at a retreat, my seminary professor challenged us to journal to God and then write what we were sensing He was saying to us.

Previously I thought of journaling as just writing to myself and that felt a little strange, but when I realized I could write prayer journals to God and then listen for His reply, it became an entirely new experience for me.

I now LOVE journaling and average about eight journals a year. As I have coached others in journaling, the method I teach is to write a letter to God and then write a letter from God. I have heard countless others say that this brought breakthrough in hearing from Him. One lady recently shared that as she practiced this technique of writing to herself from God, she was getting so many downloads that she had trouble writing fast enough.

I am confident that God wants to bring breakthrough in your walk with Him too. So I encourage you to write down what you believe you hear God saying to you. I first write God a letter where I am very honest and authentic before Him. I might include what I read in Scripture that day and if there were any challenges I felt from the Lord or any revelations or insights I want to remember. I thank Him for who He is and how good He is to me. I try to release any burdens I am still carrying and invite Him to speak into any of the problems or situations in my life concerning me. I typically ask the Lord some questions about direction I am seeking or whatever is on my mind that day. I lift up my family, the church, and the people who are on my heart asking Him to move in their lives and asking Him if there is anything that He wants to speak to me about them.

Next comes the fun part where you write a letter to yourself from God. The first time I did this, I will admit it felt a little odd because I wasn't sure if God would speak or if it would feel like me making up something to say to myself. My seminary professor encouraged us just to try it with an open mind and ask God to speak, so I decided to go for it. I started with my name at the top of the paper and then just asked the Lord what He wanted to say to me that day.

I was surprised at how natural it felt to write what I believed God was saying to me and how it even felt in a different tone than I typically write. A good portion of the letter is often encouragement from God about how much He loves me or how He is with me in whatever circumstance I am experiencing. He will often bring to mind Scriptures that He speaks over me and into my current struggles or questions. Sometimes I will hear a specific answer to something that I have been asking Him, but I have been reminded that my primary purpose in spending time with God is not to receive information or get answers. My primary calling is to know Him and to walk with Him and out of this relationship will come all that I need to know, including where He is leading me.

After you finish journaling time, it is important to remember to submit everything back to God. I always ask Him if I misheard or wrote anything that was not from Him to make it clear or to redirect me. Just like anything else you hear from God any other way, it is important to test the word and take it through the filters that I will address in the following chapters of this book: seeing if it lines up with Scripture, testing it through the godly counsel in your life, and examining whether you feel the peace of God about the direction you heard. You will have an opportunity to try two-way journaling as a part of the forty-day challenge of The Experiment.

> **Devo Time**
>
> A devo time is what I call my daily devotional time with God. That is a block of time that I set aside to spend in worship, prayer and Bible study. The simple steps I outlined in this chapter for study of the Word of God will be a core part of your devo time and help you download God's specific message for you. We will talk more about having a devo time throughout this book and give you detailed instructions and a structure to follow in The Experiment—40 Days of Hearing God's Voice Workbook.
>
> The Bible is meant to propel you into conversation with God, so keep the conversation going even after your official devo time. Some of my best revelations have come in the middle of my day when God drops an idea in my mind or speaks something to me in reply to what I asked earlier or what I read in Scripture. As you keep the communication lines open, He delights to speak!

MARK IT UP!

I once heard that a Bible that is falling apart usually belongs to a person that is not, so I make it my personal goal to mark up my Bibles by highlighting, writing, and pouring over their pages. In fact I write my annual goals on a piece of paper and tape it in the front cover of my Bible every year. I write every time that God speaks something really specific to me or gives me significant direction for my life in the back of my Bible.

I recommend marking up your Bibles because you can look back through the pages and see all the ways that God has met you. God wants to build a personal history with you through His Word. When God breathes on a verse or a promise, it comes alive. I like to write the date next to a passage or write down what God spoke to me through the passage, so that I can remember each encounter with God. When I am having a difficult day or feeling distant from God, I can go back to these passages where I have already dug a well and met with God. These verses often become a springboard that propels me back to Him. Besides this takes any Bible from being *God's Word* and turns it into *God's Word for you!*

If you have not encountered God in His Word in this way, ask Him to meet you there. He loves to reveal Himself to those that are hungry and speak to those that desire to hear Him. God's Word is never meant to merely be a theological book to be studied. Its primary role is to draw you closer to the Author so that you can know Him and be led by Him. Remember the story of Elijah I referenced earlier? God did not speak to Elijah in an earthquake, mighty wind, or a fire but rather a still, small voice. The reason why He uses a still, small voice is because He is close, and when you're close you only need to whisper. Get to know the Word, and you will draw close to the Author.

One of the analogies that God chose to explain the importance of His Word is to compare His Word to bread. The children of Israel walked in the desert for forty years, and there were some pretty amazing things going on out in that desert. God led them with a cloud by day and a pillar of fire by night. In addition, He miraculously provided food because there's not a lot to eat in the desert. So He caused it to rain bread, *manna* from heaven every day.

Exodus 16:4 says, "Then the Lord said to Moses, 'I will rain down bread from heaven for you. The people are to go out each day and gather enough for that day. In this way I will test them and see whether they will follow my instructions." He explained that He would do this every day to test them whether they would follow His Word.

God's role was to provide, but the Israelites had a role to play. They were to gather new *manna* every day because it would rot if they tried to keep it overnight. God's test was simple. Either they were going to be full that day or they were going to be hungry. Either they were going to gather and consume the *manna* or they were going to find themselves weak, tired, and frustrated.

I believe this passage foreshadows the relationship God invites us to have with His Word. God promises to provide spiritual food for us, but there is a significant responsibility on our part. We have to actually make the step to research and seek God through His Word daily, so we can apply His message to our lives. The test is simple. If we get to Wednesday and we're feeling a little bit overwhelmed by life, a bit frustrated by our circumstances, or perhaps a little weary and anxious, we should honestly evaluate if we have been daily seeking out and applying God's message to our circumstances.

God has daily bread that He wants to feed us from His Word. He's going to provide it at the right time and in the right way, but you and I have to set aside time to seek it out. He has a daily text message for you. Once you have asked your questions and done your research, you are ready to move on to step three and four in the scientific method: constructing and testing your hypothesis.

FREE RESOURCES

Send an email to resources@contactexperiment.com or visit http://ContactExperiment.com/resources to receive these bonuses:

- "Using Contact in Your Daily Life": An exclusive interview with Dr. Stine on how he applies the principles of *Contact* on a daily basis, and how you can too.

- "Contact, The Practical Science of Hearing from God": Exclusive video sermon presented by Dr. Stine.

"There are two possible outcomes: if the result confirms the hypothesis, then you've made a measurement. If the result is contrary to the hypothesis, then you've made a discovery."[19]

Enrico Fermi, Italian Physicist

"Let the wise listen and add to their learning, and let the discerning get guidance." (Proverbs 1:5)

In the scientific method, step three is to construct a hypothesis—an educated guess about how something will work. It is based on the question(s) asked in step one and the research gleaned in step two. It is called an educated guess because it is merely a prediction of the answer to the question based on your research. In your elementary school bean experiment, the hypothesis was that if you stuck a seed in some dirt, watered it daily and exposed it to the warmth of a heat lamp, the seed would sprout and become a bean plant.

In *Contact: The Practical Science of Hearing from God*, the hypothesis is what you believe God is speaking to you. As you posed your question(s) to the Lord in step one, and listened for His voice and direction, and as you further discovered His direction through your research in the written Word of God, you came up with an idea of what He is speaking to you and what He desires you to do—with the expectation that your obedience to His direction will result in certain outcomes.

Before you launch out on what you believe God is speaking to you, or if you still remain uncertain of His direction—even after following steps one and two—I encourage you to share your hypothesis with one or two close friends. In addition to speaking through the still, small voice and His Word, another primary way that God speaks is through other people. Sharing with others what you believe God is speaking to you, and allowing them to give you feedback, correlates with step four in the scientific method, which is to test your hypothesis by doing an experiment. This step is absolutely key and is one of the most missed steps in the process of hearing from God.

A scientist would never stop a science experiment at step three with just a hypothesis, so why do we stop here when we think we have heard from God? There are still steps left in the process that I believe help to build our confidence in what God is saying!

A Prophetic Word

My first job out of college was as youth pastor in the little town of DeRidder, Louisiana. I knew I was called to full-time ministry and desired to go to seminary, but I had no idea how I would ever pay for it. An opportunity presented itself for me to build a house, although there was no way that I could afford to build a house on my $12,000 a year youth pastor salary, but my dad offered to cosign the loan with me.

I kept praying that God would clearly show me if it was something I should move forward with and to shut the door

A Prophetic Word (cont.)

if it was not. On the Sunday before I needed to decide, I prayed the whole forty-five minute drive to church about whether I was supposed to take out the loan and build the house.

I was actually leaning against it because I started wondering if it was wise to borrow all that money. The title of the sermon was, "There is a Miracle in Your House." Through that message I was flooded with peace and knew that God was giving me His go ahead to build the house. I had no idea that it would be Taryn's and my first home. It also provided the finances for us to afford a home when we responded God's call to move to D.C. There truly was a miracle in my house. I knew God had clearly spoken to me through the message about something the pastor didn't even know I was asking God.

I love it when God speaks so definitively through someone else to answer a specific question I have asked Him. There have been numerous times similar to this when I have heard an answer to something I was praying through someone else. At first glance these incidences appear to be a coincidence, but each time I knew it was actually God speaking to me and confirming His voice.

Other times God has spoken to me through someone sharing something specific that God had spoken to them for me. These are often called prophetic words, and I absolutely love it when I receive one that resonates or speaks to me right where I am. However, prophetic words are not the primary way we should seek to hear God through other people. They

A Prophetic Word (cont.)

are usually an encouraging word of affirmation on either what God is speaking or helping to clarify what else God could be saying.

COUNSEL

The most frequent and reliable way God speaks to us through others is through relationships in our lives that Scripture calls counsel or advisors. For example, Proverbs 15:22 says, "Plans fail for lack of counsel, but with many advisors they succeed." The focus of this chapter is going to be on the importance of having counsel in our lives and how we can best position ourselves to hear from Him through these intentional and God-first relationships. One of the primary roles of counsel is to test what we believe we have heard from God to see if it resonates with others.

Why do so few people prioritize seeking out counsel as a way for God to speak to them or to confirm what they believe He has already spoken? One reason is because people are afraid that their hypothesis will be proved wrong when tested. They would rather not submit the message to trusted counsel because they want to do what they want to do without other people's input. This type of person tends to be those that use the phrase "God told me to do this" at alarmingly frequent rates and are not open to hearing another person's perspective if it disagrees with theirs. I do not think I need to elaborate on why these people are placing themselves in an unhealthy, dangerous position. Proverbs 12:15

describes them as fools because they are *not* seeking *or* heeding counsel, "The way of a fool is right in his own eyes but he who heeds counsel is wise."[20]

I had an individual come to my office a few years ago claiming to be seeking counsel. After entering the room, he sat down on my couch and proceeded to tell me that God had spoken to him and that he knew what he was going to do in the situation—even though he was supposedly coming to me to seek my advice. When I asked him why he made the appointment, he said, "Well, the Bible says that I am supposed to seek counsel." I asked him, "If I told you that I didn't think you should move forward in the situation, would you change your mind or course of action? He answered with a frank but adamant "No." This man was not coming to seek counsel. He was coming to communicate information in hopes that I would agree with him, so he could check off what he felt was the obligatory "seeking counsel."

There are many like this man who honestly do not want counsel. However, I believe the most common reason that people do not submit what they heard to counsel is that they have never *chosen* people to play this role in their life. They either skip this step entirely or they end up asking a plethora of people whom they are not in close relationship with or who do not have a biblical worldview. It is no surprise that they end up getting confused when "their counsel" gives different advice.

They often misuse Proverbs 11:14 which says, "Where there is no counsel, the people fall; but in the multitude of counselors there is safety."[21]

WISE COUNSEL

Proverbs 11:14 says to seek counsel through a multitude of counselors, but when we look at the Hebrew word for counsel we receive a vital barometer to use when selecting our counsel. The Hebrew word for counsel means "wise counsel or good advice and direction" and the Hebrew word for counselors means those that "counsel or give wise advice."

This verse is not saying to choose just any group of counselors, but those who give *wise* advice. The word for counsel is actually a Hebrew nautical term conveying that receiving and following wise advice will help steer us in the right direction. Therefore, it is paramount who we choose to speak into our life because this verse reminds us that when we choose well, we will find safety. So how do we find wise counsel?

I have three preliminary questions I use as a litmus test:

One: Are they walking closely with God?

The first question I ask, "Are they walking closely with God?" is the most important question. Proverbs 11:14 says we need to have those that will give us wise advice and that comes best from those that have a vibrant relationship with God and that make decisions with a biblical worldview.

Having a vibrant relationship with God means they spend time with God and hear from Him. I want to receive counsel from someone who is listening to His leading both for their life *and* for my life.

I define a biblical worldview as one that looks to the Word of God as their ultimate truth and authority, which means that their value system lines up with God's value system. This manifests in their life through their personal character, their genuine love for people, and their desire to live life for what ultimately matters— eternity.

Two: Are they walking closely with me?

The second question, "Are they walking closely with me?" is also very important because I have found that the people who can give me the best advice are the people who know me the very best. They know my strengths, weakness, fears, dreams, and insecurities, so they have insight into my life that others would miss. They also are praying for me on a regular basis and have a vested interest in my life so they *are* trusted counselors whose words have weight and authority in my life.

Three: Are they able to tell me "no"?

The third question, "Are they able to tell me no?" is one that is often missed. If you surround yourself with those that will automatically agree with you, often referred to as "yes men," you are missing the whole point of seeking counsel. You need to give people permission to tell you "no" and take the time to listen to why they disagree with you or have reservations about your ideas. Those closest to you often have a different vantage point that is able to bring to light something that you missed seeing, and even save you from future trouble. Proverbs 19:20 says, "Listen to advice and accept discipline, and at the end you will be counted among the wise." Are you willing to hear advice or discipline, even when it is not what you want to hear, and take time to seriously weigh what has been shared?

Someone who was not afraid to give me straightforward advice and even provide some needed discipline in my life was Billy Hornsby. Billy was one of the founders of the Association of Related Churches (ARC), an organization that helps plant churches all over the world, who became a mentor and personal friend. He was one of the kindest, most fun-loving men you could ever meet, but he was also not afraid to speak the truth. I learned this firsthand when he came to visit DC Metro about a year after we planted the church. He evaluated every aspect of our services and of the DC Metro experience and he gave us a C-. Yes, only slightly better than a D. Ouch! I admit this was a tough pill to swallow because he was a man I deeply respected, and I wanted him to be impressed with the ministry we were developing in our nation's capital.

However, looking back, I am thankful for his brutal honesty, because he gave me a list of ten things he would change. For example, he said we needed to train our leaders on how to host guests because his travel experience was subpar. He advised us to remove superfluous parts of the service that non-Christians and new believers would not understand and recommended adding a ten-minute guest reception at the end of each service to be able to connect with those that were new to the church. We implemented every one of his recommendations and saw immediate fruit, especially in our guest relations. After his assessment, we were compelled to study the organizations with the best guest relations in the world to find the ones that we would model ourselves after: The Ritz-Carlton, Nordstrom, and Starbucks.

I am happy to say that when Billy returned a year later, he gave his experience at DC Metro an A. The only significant feedback he recommended on his second visit was that I take my family on a vacation because we needed some rest and quality time together. He also challenged me to intentionally invest in a relationship with another ARC church planter whose church was at a similar stage as DC Metro.

My first thought was Pastor Rob Brendle from Denver United. What I didn't know is that Billy had told Pastor Rob something similar. At Billy's bidding, we both began to invest in our relationship, and Rob quickly became a close friend. He actually took Billy's place on our board, as one of DC Metro's overseers when Billy passed away. I am incredibly thankful for Billy's willingness to give me honest feedback and to challenge me because it is still bearing fruit in my life and in DC Metro today. Do you have these types of relationships in your life? If not, I believe that it is God's desire to help you find them.

S.A.F.E. RELATIONSHIPS

A recent study indicated that the greatest statistical predictor of spiritual growth is the quantity of close Christian friends a person has in any given season of his or her life. In other words, from a statistical growth standpoint, having healthy, God-first friendships is far more important than any other Christian behavior or discipline. Peter Haas, founder and lead pastor of Substance Church in Minneapolis, elaborates on these findings, "Research found that you can preach the same quantity of God's Word to two different people, and studies show that the 'person with more close Christian friends' is the one who is 'most likely to apply it.'"[22]

This study reinforces our DC Metro small group motto, "Transformation happens best in the context of healthy, God-first relationships." We believe healthy God-first relationships are S.A.F.E. relationships, meaning that they are:

Supportive—We are called to support and encourage one another, after all, we all need friends who will be there for us in the good times and hard times.

Accountable—We need people in our life that we can be totally authentic with and who sharpen us and, no matter what, point us back to Christ.

Fun—We need people in our life that we can enjoy and who help us live the abundant life God calls us to enjoy *together*.

Empowering—We are called to speak into one another's lives and help each other fulfill our God-given purpose and potential in life.

I intentionally place S.A.F.E. relationships in my life not only because they enrich my life and have helped me become who I am called to be, but also because they play the vital role of providing me trusted, godly counsel.

_S_upportive

The people you place as counsel in your life should play a supportive, encouraging role in the narrative of your life. As I mentioned when I shared the three questions I ask when choosing counsel, they are people that should know you well and love you because this gives them more authority and insight to speak into your life. They will sacrifice for you and help support you so that you can accomplish more together than you could possibly accomplish apart.

Ecclesiastes 4:9-12 describes the advantages of this type of unified, synergistic relationship:

> Two are better than one, because they have a good return for their labor; If either of them falls down, one can help the other up. But pity anyone who falls and has no one to help them up. Also, if two lie down together, they will keep warm. But how can one keep warm alone? Though one may be overpowered, two can defend themselves. A cord of three strands is not quickly broken.

This passage reminds me of Bubba's relationship with Forest Gump when he stated; "I'm gonna lean up against you, you just lean right back against me. This way, we don't have to sleep with our heads in the mud. You know why we a good partnership,

Forrest? 'Cause we be watchin' out for one another. Like brothers and stuff."[23] Our lives get real muddy when we attempt to go it alone. Jethro modeled this type of supportive relationship to Moses in Exodus 18. Even though Moses had received the best education available in Egypt, I believe he learned even more from Jethro about practical leadership. Jethro taught Moses how he could serve the people more strategically. After heeding Jethro's advice, Moses became a much better leader of the people, and better sustainer of his own life.

Jethro knew Moses had a tendency to try to please people because he understood his weaknesses. Jethro told Moses that there was no way Moses could continue to handle the number of people that wanted to see him every day without growing too weary. Jethro played a vital role in Moses' life by speaking *into* Moses' life and coming up with a practical solution to an issue affecting his success as a leader. We all need people in our lives that help us see our blind spots and support us by figuring out practical ways that we can overcome our current obstacles.

Accountable

The people we place as counsel in our lives also have a role of accountability. As we agree to be authentic with them and give them permission to speak into our lives, they bring great affirmation of the road ahead. The overseers of DC Metro are some who play this role in my life because I openly share with them when I am walking through a challenge. However, the two people that play this role in the greatest way are my wife Taryn and my best friend, Matt. I have allowed them access to every area of my life, and have agreed to be transparent with them in any area of struggle. Although sometimes a bit humbling and even embarrassing, I have found it to also be one of the most freeing disciplines in life.

When we confess our sins to each other and share our insecurities and fears, we are actually deepening our relationship with the other person. We are showing them that they are someone that we value and trust enough to share the parts of our self that are not *open to the public.* I have found that transparency begets transparency, so if I open up and share first, I am also providing a safe place where they can be themselves and share openly about their shortcomings and insecurities. No matter how embarrassing or how revealing, this type of open transparency brings safety.

James 5:16 instructs, "Therefore confess your sins to each other and pray for each other so that you may be healed. The prayer of a righteous person is powerful and effective." The Greek word for <u>healed</u> in this passage can be translated as "physical healing," but it can also mean "healing of the soul." I have found both to be true in my own life, especially the healing of the soul, which is comprised of our *mind, will,* and *emotions.*

In James 5:16, we are instructed to "pray for each other" which is written in the present imperative and translates as "pray and keep on praying for each other." We are able to serve one another by being a reflection of God's heart to each other in the midst of our brokenness and by praying for each other when we share our failures. There is something powerful that takes place as you show yourself as you really are which leads to receiving unconditional love.

Recently, my son Isaac grabbed a book from seminary days off my bookshelf. It was about the healing power of community called *The Safest Place on Earth*. As I began reading it again, I began to see how timely it was that Isaac should "happen" to pick up this particular book because it confirmed what God had been teaching me. This book provoked me to be even more transparent in my closest relationships.

In this book, Larry Crabb explains, "A central task of community is to create a safe enough place for walls to be torn down... In spiritual community, people reach deep places in each other's hearts that are not often or easily reached. They openly express love and reveal fear even though they are not accustomed to that level of intimacy. When they reach a sacred place of vulnerability and authenticity, something is released. Something good begins to happen."[24]

It's amazing when we experience true Christian friendship the way Christ intended it to be. The results are all together transformative to our soul. If you have yet to experience this—I challenge you—be vulnerable and open up to a safe person: the results will leave you desiring more.

Fun

I personally believe that the people who you place as closest counsel in your life should be those you have fun with and enjoy. I will be the first to admit that at first glance many pastors would not have fun as one of their top qualifications for counsel, but I definitely recommend this quality. Most Americans have a tendency to overwork and consequently their life becomes unbalanced, with their personal life and fun taking a backseat to their careers. I don't believe this is God's design for us, as He desires us to have life-giving relationships as a top priority in our lives.

First of all, I believe you should sincerely enjoy the people you have in the closest places in your life. I have had the same best friends for almost fifteen years. We vacation together, we have dinner parties together, and we celebrate birthdays/life's milestones together. Simply put, we have a ridiculous amount of fun together. Just like in a marriage, I believe you need to be intentional about doing activities that you enjoy together and that you need to be purposeful about having fun. I want those who are speaking into my life to know what makes my heart come alive, what makes me laugh, and what brings me the deepest joy. After all, as C.S. Lewis wrote, "Joy is the serious business of heaven."[25]

Second, I want to receive from people who are living the life that Jesus promised in John 10:10, "I came that they may have life, and have it to the full." I purposefully seek out those who know how to live to the fullest and who help me live this *carpe diem* lifestyle. Whoever said God is boring and that our lives as Christians have to be dull has not had a true revelation of Him. God is the most enjoyable being that has ever existed, and I want to be around those that remind me of this reality. After all, life and ministry is meant to be a fun and fulfilling adventure with God.

Some may argue that fun is too hedonistic of a barometer, but I have found the most profound joy actually comes from serving Jesus, doing life with other believers, and being a part of others' lives being transformed. This is the type of fun I am talking about and what I seek to share with those who play the role of my closest friends and advisors. I think we could all use a little more fun in our lives, after all walking out God's call on our life is meant to be an enjoyable group project.

Empowering

The counsel in your life should also be empowering. We talked about biblical accountability earlier. We tend to focus on areas of sin or weakness when we think of accountability but true biblical accountability also includes empowerment. You are holding the people closest in your life accountable to the dreams that are in their heart and to walking in the gifts and passions you see in their life. You hold them accountable to be who God has called them to be and do anything you can to empower them or push them toward their calling in life.

Empowering is one of my favorite roles to play with those that are on our executive leadership team. A couple of years ago we were out to lunch as a lead team. Dr. Joseph Umidi, the current dean of Regent University's School of Divinity, and one of our DC Metro overseers, shared with us what he believed was the main reason why DC Metro had grown at a significant rate and yet remained spiritually healthy: our relationships with each other. Dr. Umidi called our relationships our _secret sauce_ because they are what the Holy Spirit flows through to reveal the deep, unconditional love of God.

I began to unpack Dr. Umidi's statement as I looked at the people around the table. Most of the members of the lead team I have known for over a decade. We have walked through each other's trials as well as each other's great victories. We know each other's weaknesses and vulnerabilities, but we also know how to call forth the best in each other. We know beyond a shadow of a doubt that we are for each other and that we are better together than we would be apart. I believe that God desires these types of relationships in each of our lives. C.S. Lewis explains:

> In friendship...we think we have chosen our peers. In reality a few years' difference in the dates of our births, a few more miles between certain houses, the choice of one university instead of another...the accident of a topic being raised or not raised at a first meeting–any of these chances might have kept us apart. But, for a Christian, there are, strictly speaking, no chances. A secret master of ceremonies has been at work. Christ, who said to the disciples, "You have not chosen me, but I have chosen you," can truly say to every group of Christian friends, "You have not chosen one another but I have chosen you *for* one another."[26]

I know God strategically placed each of the people who are in the closest places in my life, but it has taken intentionality on my part to invest in these relationships. If you do not already have these S.A.F.E relationships in your life, I believe that God wants to help you develop them. It is a strategic way that He wants to speak to you. If you do have these relationships, I encourage you to continue to invest in them and ask God to help you recognize His voice through them. They are truly your greatest assets in this life.

BONDS AND BOATS

In seminary, I experienced the honor of someone I deeply respect seeking counsel from me when my dad informed me he found a sailboat he was interested in purchasing. After many years of casually looking at boats, this particular boat had captured his attention enough that he asked me to pray about whether he should buy it—he was unsure if he should spend money on a recreational expense.

It is important to mention that my dad is extremely thrifty, and he actually had the money in a savings account from an insurance reimbursement he had received years earlier when his old boat was destroyed in a Louisiana hurricane. In my mind, I thought he should buy the boat because he has always had a passion for sailing, and he had the money sitting in a bank account. However, because I knew how unlike it was for my frugal dad to buy anything that he considered frivolous, I told him I would pray that God would confirm whether he should buy the boat. Little did I know how incredibly God would answer that prayer.

When I entered the campus prayer chapel—a routine of mine each day before hitting the books in the library—I had two main requests I was lifting up to God. The first was my dad's boat and the second was my need for additional finances for living expenses while I was in seminary. At the time I had a series of part-time jobs, but it was still a stretch each month to pay all my bills. My roommate Matt and I were living off of hot dogs and mac-and-cheese, so I decided I would ask God for help.

After about half an hour talking with God, and right before I was getting ready to leave, I heard God say, "Sell the bonds and I'll give him the boat." This phrase was honestly baffling to me because I did not know what bonds He was talking about—even though I knew it was His voice.

I was asking God what He meant when I suddenly remembered that my parents had told me years earlier that they had purchased savings bonds for me when I was born. I also remembered that a week earlier my mom had sent me an old accordion file containing papers and documents from my childhood. When I received this file, I had stuck it in my closet giving no thought to what it contained.

I decided to skip my time in the library that afternoon to go on a little adventure with God. On my drive home, I was wondering if that old file could possibly contain the savings bonds my parents had bought for me a quarter of a century ago. I was thrilled when I pulled the accordion file from the closet to find a dusty manila envelope with the savings bonds that had matured only one month prior. However, nothing could have prepared me for what else I would pull out of that same manila envelope.

In that same envelope was a brochure for a sailboat that I had picked up at a marina in Louisiana and placed in the file years earlier. I know...what are the odds? Well, it gets even better. I pulled out the brochure for the sailboat to find out it was for a 1997 Hunter twenty-five foot sailboat, which was the exact make, model and year that my dad was looking at! In my left hand, I was holding the savings bonds and in my right hand, I was holding the brochure. I was so blown away I could hardly contain myself at the specificity and goodness of God.

The phrase, "Sell the bonds and I'll give him the boat" reverberated in my head as now it made perfect sense. Of course, I immediately called my dad and told him that I felt very confident that God wanted him to buy the boat. God knew it was hard for my dad to buy things for himself, so He wanted to do something so overt that no one could doubt that God wanted Him to buy a boat. God knew I was struggling financially and that He would lead me to the bonds right after they matured at the exact time I was in need of finances.

As my father sought out my counsel on his desire to purchase a boat, God confirmed his decision to me as I prayed, and through the unique circumstances of the bonds and the boat brochure. Not only was I able to affirm his decision in my counsel, but God used the situation to meet my financial needs.

As incredible as it was for my dad to get the sailboat he had been dreaming about and for me to get the financial resources I needed, we received something far more valuable that day. We heard the voice of God in an undeniable way, which became a powerful reminder of how much He loves us and how He is involved in the intricate details of our life. We still marvel at the kindness of God and how we believe He had been planning that surprise for us since my parents first bought the bonds twenty-five years earlier.

CHOOSING YOUR COUNSEL

By seeking council in life as you attempt to hear from God you will truly fulfill the scientific method of the practical science of hearing God's voice. Testing your hypothesis by inviting others to weigh in on what you believe God is speaking to you will prove to be a final confirmation or a S.A.F.E. redirection as His voice is clarified.

In the accompanying workbook, *The Experiment—40 Days of Hearing God's Voice Workbook* we are going to ask you to share what God speaks to you as you spend thirty minutes with Him each day for forty days. In preparation, think of one relationship that you have that is a good candidate for being wise counsel for you. Remember, I define wise counsel as a person who is walking closely with God and with you, and who will not be afraid to tell you "no" if they do not agree with what you believe God is saying.

Is the individual you have in mind a S.A.F.E. relationship? Are they supportive, will they provide accountability, are they fun and empowering? If your answer to all the above questions is "yes," give them a call and schedule a time to meet.

During your meeting, share with your friend the purpose of The Experiment.

- Give them a summary of *Contact: The Practical Science of Hearing from God* and how you are applying the steps of the scientific method to learning to hear and discern the voice of God.

- Explain where they fit into the process as a person you trust, that you can share what you believe God is speaking to you.

- Tell them the definition you learned of wise counsel, and what a S.A.F.E. relationship is. Tell them why you picked them for the role.

- If they agree to fill the role, pray together that God would bless the relationship, and give them wisdom and discernment.

- Share with them what you have been asking God and the answers you believe God has spoken to you through your prayer and study.

- Remember no counsel you choose will give you perfect advice or hear from the Lord perfectly. If your counsel does not believe you should move forward in what you shared, it is worth investing some significant time in prayer and asking them to continue to pray too.

- Don't do all the talking. After you have spoken, allow your friend the freedom to ask questions and share their ideas and counsel.

You have asked God your question(s) and done research in the Word of God—looking for answers to your questions or confirmation of the answers you already received. You have submitted your hypothesis of what you believe God is speaking to you to trusted counsel from other individuals. Now it's time to move on to Step Five of the scientific method: analyzing and drawing a conclusion about what you believe God has spoken.

CHAPTER FOUR | THE ANALYSIS AND CONCLUSION

"The only relevant test of the validity of a hypothesis is comparison of prediction with experience."[27]

Milton Friedman, Economist

"Do not be anxious about anything, but in every situation, by prayer and petition, with thanksgiving, present your requests to God. And the peace of God, which transcends all understanding, will guard your hearts and your minds in Christ Jesus." (Philippians 4:6-7)

Step five of the scientific method is to analyze the data and draw a conclusion. The data is the record of what happened during the experiment. Once a scientist has completed his or her experiment, they collect and analyze the data to see if it supports the original hypothesis. Many times scientists find that their original hypothesis could not be supported by the data. Based on what they have learned from their experiments, the scientists will develop a new hypothesis. This starts the scientific method process over again.

Thomas Edison had a hypothesis of what it would take to create the light bulb. He made over a thousand attempts and filled over forty thousand pages of notes before he found the missing piece that led him to invent the light bulb. Edison was searching for the right material for the filament, the little wire inside the light bulb.

"'Before I got through,' Edison recalled, 'I tested no fewer than 6,000 vegetable growths, and ransacked the world for the most suitable filament material.'"[28] His attempts included coconut fiber, fishing line and even hairs from a friend's beard, before Edison finally figured out to use carbonized bamboo for the filament.[29]

Patent number 223,898 was given to Edison's electric bulb, which was one of 1,093 patents accredited to Thomas Edison.[30] Edison reflected on his piece de resistance, "The electric light has caused me the greatest amount of study and has required the most elaborate experiments...We are striking it big in the electric light, better than my vivid imagination first conceived. Where this thing is going to stop, Lord only knows."[31] Thankfully Edison did not give up on searching for the missing piece.

Edison was one of my middle school heroes. As I shared, I incessantly dreamed of one day having a patent in my name. In fact, in my quest to win at the science fair, I tried the same experiment with magnets four times and entered in four different science fairs. Each time I attempted to make a metal ball levitate by wrapping coils around nails to create a magnetic pull strong enough to keep the ball floating in mid-air.

Each year it was an epic fail, so I hypothesized that I needed more power and tried to add a stronger magnetic pull each successive year. Ironically, even though my science experiment failed again and again, my final year I still won the science fair for explaining why my hypothesis was wrong. My missing piece was power. I am sorry to say that unlike Edison, I did not have the tenacity to keep trying after the fourth failed attempt, so the missing piece remained, "missing."

FINDING THE "MISSING PEACE"

Have you ever had a missing piece that you desperately needed to make something work? Nothing can be more frustrating than having a missing piece to a puzzle or a final part of a solution to an issue.

When it comes to hearing the voice of God and discerning which direction to step, I have found that there is a final piece that simply cannot remain missing, which is the *peace of God*. One of the first questions I ask myself when I am contemplating taking a step in a certain direction is, "Do I have peace?" If I believe I have heard God through His still, small voice, His Word or through counsel, I always test it with whether I feel peace.

At first, the litmus test of whether I feel peace about the situation or direction can seem too subjective or too dependent on mood. That is until you understand that a biblical definition of peace is much more than a feeling and is one of the primary ways that He confirms where He is leading. As the next step in *Contact: The Practical Science of Hearing from God*, analyzing the data and drawing a conclusion is used to evaluate the direction we have received from the Lord, but at the end of the day, I do not move forward without His peace.

A BIBLICAL UNDERSTANDING OF PEACE

The word peace is mentioned 400 times throughout Scripture and has several different connotations. The first connotation describes a believer's state of reconciliation with God because of what Jesus did on the cross. Romans 5:1 says, "Therefore, since we have been justified through faith, *we have peace with God through our Lord Jesus Christ.*"

The second connotation of peace describes the type of relationship God desires us to have with others. Talking about this type of relational peace, Romans 12:18 states "as far as it depends on you, *live at peace with everyone.*"

The third connotation of peace is the one that we are going to be focusing on in this chapter. It is listed as the third fruit of the Spirit in Galatians 5:22 and is described in Philippians 4:7, "The peace of God, which transcends all understanding, will guard your hearts and your minds in Christ Jesus."

The Greek word for <u>peace</u> means "harmony or tranquility." But as Philippians 4:7 explains, this peace is supernatural and beyond rational comprehension. This Greek word should be understood as "not just freedom from trouble, but everything that makes for a man's highest good"[32] and relates to the Hebrew word for peace, *shalom*, which has a basic meaning of "totality or completeness including fulfillment, maturity, soundness, and wholeness."[33]

Let's look at a few other verses that describe this supernatural peace to further understand this gift that God gives to believers as we submit ourselves to His leadership. Isaiah 26:3 says, "You will *keep in perfect peace* those whose minds are steadfast, because they trust in you." In other words, peace is promised for those who trust in Him. Isaiah 55:12 explains "you shall go out in joy, and be *led forth in peace.*" Joy and peace are gifts from the Lord as we follow Him. In John 14:27, Jesus again promises His supernatural peace to believers, "Peace I leave with you; *my peace I give you.* I do not give you as the world gives. Do not let your hearts be troubled and do not be afraid." It is evident that this peace does not come from the absence of trials or problems but rather comes from the presence of God with you no matter what you are walking through or where you go.

What about my emotions?

Have you noticed that your emotions are not particularly trustworthy? In fact, depending on what is happening in your life, your emotions can be like a rollercoaster—way up one moment and way down the next, not to mention when they take you on a ride around in loops. While your feelings are a normal part of your human nature, and not to be suppressed or denied, be careful that you don't let them take the lead in your life, as they can take you places you don't want to go.

When I talk about the peace of God, I am not talking about your feelings. The peace of God is something that transcends your human emotions and rational comprehension. There is an old gospel song that talks about God giving peace in the midst of the storm. The idea is that in the middle of turmoil and chaos (the storm) God can give a supernatural peace that everything will somehow be alright. Your rollercoaster of emotions in the storm may include fear, anxiety or dread, but somehow the peace of God overrides all the emotions and gives you the grace to trust in Him.

While the peace of God can have a calming effect on your emotions, it is not given to you through your emotions, but by the Holy Spirit to your human spirit. That's why

> *What about my emotions? (cont.)*
>
> Philippians 4:6-7 tells us not to be anxious about anything (emotion), but tell God our needs, and thank Him for meeting our needs (spirit to Spirit communication with God), and the result will be His peace—deposited in our human spirit—guarding our heart and mind.
>
> If you haven't got it completely sorted out what is your emotions and what is His peace, don't worry. Your ability to discern between His peace and your emotions will increase as you grow in your relationship to Him.

THE PEACE OF GOD GUIDES US

So how does peace relate to God's guidance? Colossians 3:15 gives us further insight, "let the *peace of God rule in your hearts*."[34] In the Amplified Bible, the word rule is defined as "act as an umpire." Just as an umpire decides whether a play is safe, fair, or good, so the peace of God is to act as an umpire in the decisions we make. The Good News Translation of this same verse says, "The peace that Christ gives is to guide you in the decisions you make."

Sometimes I know God has been leading me to make decisions that do not seem completely logical, but they are accompanied by what I can only describe as supernatural peace. I felt God's presence strongly with me, which manifested as the peace that passes all understanding that Paul referred to in Philippians 4:7.

One of these times was when God called Taryn and I to move across the country to start DC Metro Church. I was an associate pastor at an incredible church I loved—Celebration Church—in

Jacksonville, Florida. Taryn was also on staff working in the women's ministry. We thoroughly enjoyed our roles and relationships in the church. We had known for many years that God was calling us to plant a church in the D.C. Metro area one day in the future, but we did not know when He would send us, so we became very rooted in Celebration.

In November 2006, Taryn and I both began to strongly feel it was time. We met with our lead pastors and dear friends, Stovall and Kerri Weems, who agreed that it was time. We all felt God's indescribable peace, even though it made us sad to think about not doing life and ministry together. It certainly did not seem logical to leave. Our son Isaac was only a year old at the time of our move, and we had just found out that Taryn was pregnant with our second son Josiah.

We were also leaving people we loved and secure jobs in a phenomenal church—and for what, to launch out into the unknown with no income and a growing family to support? Not exactly what most financial advisors would recommend, but the remarkable part is that we felt an unwavering, supernatural peace along with the peace that came through my pastor's council and support. Now don't get me wrong, Taryn and I would look at each other sometimes and ask each other if we were crazy. However, even in the midst of our questioning, we felt an undeniable peace—a peace that truly passed all our understanding.

I have learned that unless God's presence goes with me, I do not want to go; and if His presence is leading me, then I do not want to stay. I have found that His peace is a very helpful litmus test to see if He is initiating a move, ultimately because I want to know that He is going with me.

In Exodus 33:15, Moses expressed a similar desire when God was calling him to a foreign land. He wanted to make sure the Lord understood that the only way he was going was if God went with him, "If your presence does not go with us, do not send us up from here." I felt the exact same way when we were leaving Florida, but the peace both Taryn and I felt was confirmation that God's presence was with us and that it was He who was sending us. As we stepped out in obedience, God proved to be faithful every step of the way, and He met all our needs, as we responded to His leading.

Another time God called us to step out in faith prompted by His peace was when DC Metro was moving into our first permanent facility, 1100 N Fayette Street in Alexandria, Virginia. We had been meeting in the movie theater for over two years, and we really wanted to find a building that could become our permanent church home. On Easter Sunday morning in 2009, I was driving my normal route from Starbucks to the movie theater that we called home, when I stumbled upon a building that was for lease directly in my path. I immediately fell in love with the building as I could picture it as a church where thousands of people would encounter God and be changed in His presence.

I began to pursue leasing this building, but I was extremely discouraged when I heard the price. After some quick mental math, I realized that our church income would have to double to afford the building. In my rational, business mind that was an immediate "no." However, to my surprise, I had an incredibly strong peace about the building. I began to seek counsel with our overseers and our leadership team. To my astonishment again, every single one said they felt peace too and thought we should lease the building.

Even though part of me was quite nervous, the peace we felt was stronger, so we signed the lease to move into the building. I shared in an earlier chapter that the month we signed the lease our church income doubled! God came through for us in a way that confirmed that His hand was definitely upon our bold step of faith. We experienced firsthand what Paul was referring to in Romans 15:13, "May the God of hope fill you with all joy and peace as you trust in him, so that you may overflow with hope by the power of the Holy Spirit."

When God is guiding you in a decision or path that does not seem logical or causes you to step outside of your comfort zone, He gives you His peace to remind you just as He told Moses in Exodus 33:14, "My presence will go with you."

What about the real tough times?

Life is often difficult. God never promised us that every day would be easy. We face circumstances where our world is being shaken, where challenges and conflicts leave us numb without natural peace, and the human emotional response is fear, sorrow, pain or any number of other feelings. Sometimes the tough seasons in life are due to our bad choices, other people's bad choices or even the devil's attack, but regardless of the cause of the trial, God promises to walk through it with us.

Jesus is our example. The will of God for His life was full of conflict with religious and political leaders, confrontations

What about the real tough times? (cont.)

with demons, and climaxed in His death on the Cross. We know that His humanity experienced the full range of human emotions—He struggled. In the Garden of Gethsemane He told his disciples that He was "deeply distressed and troubled. 'My soul is overwhelmed with sorrow to the point of death'" (Mark 14:33-34). He prayed three separate times asking God to remove the cup of suffering that He was about to experience. Luke's version of the story tells us that he was in anguish, praying so hard His sweat was like drops of blood falling to the ground (that is some serious praying). While Jesus was honest with His emotions, His prayer was ultimately one of submission to the will of His Father: "yet not my will, but yours be done" (Luke 22:42).

Did Jesus experience a supernatural peace that surpassed His raging emotions—the Bible is silent about that. What we do know is that after He had wrestled with His emotions in prayer—three times—He was ready to move forward in the will of God (the scourging, mocking, and the agony of the Cross). My point? When you are called to difficult circumstances in life where a natural peace is lacking, deal honestly with your emotions before God, submit yourself fully to the will of God, and move forward in the will of God. As you do that, trust that God can deposit a supernatural peace in your spirit that will surpass the thoughts in your mind and your rollercoaster emotions.

LOSING AND REGAINING YOUR PEACE

One question I am often asked is what to do if you had peace at one point, and then you lose it. Peace gives us an initial green light to take a first step but sometimes we lose our peace along the way. There are different reasons we can lose our peace. We may have let fear creep in so that we are no longer being led by faith but rather by our emotions and insecurities. If this is the case, don't derail the process but instead go back to the place you first had peace.

This is exactly what happened to me when we were buying our first house in the D.C. area. We found a neighborhood we loved in the school district we wanted for our kids, so we began the search. One morning during that season, I was reading Ephesians 5, when I felt the Holy Spirit highlight verse 25, "Husbands, love your wives, just as Christ loved the church and gave Himself up for her." This is a sweet sentimental sounding verse that is read at many weddings, but I have been walking with the Lord long enough to know that when God highlights a verse like this, it is often because He is going to give me an opportunity to walk it out.

I was right. Almost immediately after reading that verse, I sensed the still, small voice of God whisper to let Taryn pick out the house we would buy. I consented to this prompting but I must admit I was feeling rather prideful about what a good husband I was to let her choose the house. I felt like I deserved a big pat on the back. One of my passions is picking, purchasing and renovating houses, but I was going to obey the passage in Ephesians and lay down my life and choices for my wife.

Taryn was elated when I told her she could pick the house. She quickly found a ranch-style house in our favorite neighborhood, but as soon as we pulled up to tour the house, I completely lost my peace. The landscaping was ridiculously overgrown. When we stepped inside, the house reeked of a foul odor. I am still not quite sure what to say about the seventies wall paper or décor. Not to mention there was a dripping sound coming from the basement. I went downstairs to check it out only to find chains hanging from the ceiling. My immediate thought was we must have stumbled upon an axe murderer hang out.

I looked over at Taryn to give her the "let's get out of here" look only to find my wife's eyes lit up. I thought, *Uh oh, I know that look...she likes it.* My wife is an incredible visionary, and she began to cast vision about our future home, "David, we can *blow this wall out* and *this wall out* and *we can renovate this area.*"

I must confess at that point all I could see were dollar bill signs flashing before my eyes. With each new project she proposed, my peace seemed to dissipate further and further at an alarming rate.

I began to dialogue with the Lord; *I can't believe she likes this house? The renovations she wants to do will cost a small fortune and the house already costs more than it is worth in my opinion. This does not feel peaceful!* The Lord asked me when the last time I had peace was. I thought back to the conversation when I told Taryn she could pick the house after God spoke to me though Ephesians 5. I quickly realized that I had tried to take control of picking the house again when the last time God had spoken to me was to let Taryn choose. I repented and released the decision back to Taryn, and immediately my peace came rushing back. I still was not happy about the house and still did not think it was the best deal, but I had peace that God was with us in the decision.

Taryn had no idea of the internal dialogue I had just had with the Lord, but she turned to me and said, "I don't think we should buy this house." My wife is a savvy businesswoman and when she crunched the numbers, she concluded that it was overpriced. "I love the house. I have a vision for it, but I don't think the numbers make sense," she said. Secretly I was thrilled. End of story...or so I thought.

The next day Taryn was back on the MLS, and she realized the owners of the ranch-style house had dropped the price by seventy-thousand dollars. We prayed about it again and both felt a green light and tremendous peace. All of the qualities that I didn't like about the house at first were cosmetic and easily altered, particularly because we were able to invest the money from the price drop into the needed renovations. The house became a home where we had many happy memories. When we sold it, we even gained a significant profit. This became yet another testimony of the wisdom of following God's peace and how to regain it even when you lose it.

GOD'S REDEMPTION

I have had to follow this process of restoring peace in my own life countless times, but I have found that even when we step off course, God loves to draw us back and brings the needed redemption. There is no place that I have seen this more clearly than my relationship with my wife. We were engaged—twice.

I met Taryn at a college conference in Baton Rouge, Louisiana and was immediately drawn to her. I prayed with my prayer partner for six weeks for the opportunity to run into her again and ask her out. When I saw her at the business school, my fraternity brother asked who she was dating. I thought to myself, *me*. Ok maybe I really wasn't in that moment, but a few minutes later she said "yes" to a date. On our first date, I talked to her of my dream of starting a church in the D.C. area one day. She shared that she too had dreams of doing something great for God. My heart felt an abundance of peace, as I sensed that she could be "the one."

Fast forward three years later to a broken engagement with Taryn. Confusion and hurt usurped the peace that had previously filled my heart. Hindsight is always 20/20, but I now see that I had allowed myself to be too influenced by one person's counsel who was against us getting married. This person was not close to either of us—hence the need for the previous chapter. This person's perspective had triggered my own doubts, and the same in Taryn, which caused both of us to pull away from each other and ultimately call off our wedding.

I didn't talk with Taryn for almost a year after we ended our engagement until I decided to call her after the 9/11 tragedy to check on her. She then came to visit the graduate school I was attending in Virginia Beach as a "prospective student," and we quickly realized we still had feelings for each other. Peace came flooding back and within a few months we were engaged again.

Testing Counsel

Taryn and I got some negative counsel from a source that we didn't have a S.A.F.E. relationship with, bringing doubts about our relationship, and leading us to break off our engagement—the first time. Unfortunately, we did not weigh out the advice we were receiving, and allowed it to influence our decisions.

Even when you have the most trusted counselors in your life, and you receive the best counsel—*you* are still responsible to weigh their advice. Thessalonians 5:20-21 says, "Do not treat prophecies with contempt, but test them all and hold onto that which is good?" All prophecies (words of encouragement, comfort or direction) and advice from others need to be weighed. What is the spirit in which the advice is given? What are the consequences of following the advice—where will it lead?

Sometimes the only way to weigh the counsel of others is the test of time. Not discounting what has been spoken to you, but holding it lightly before God until He confirms the advice, or proves it wrong. You and I are to be open to counsel, but we are not to roll over and accept everything that someone speaks over us, or to us—even godly people. God calls us to be responsible, testing words and holding to that which is good.

We now understand that the confusion we were feeling that had caused us to break off our engagement was not actually the lack of God's peace. The peace was just buried underneath all of the other soulish emotions that we allowed to dictate our choices. God, in His mercy, allowed us to be reunited, and we were married the next summer. One of Taryn's favorite parts of our story is that when she went to a bridal boutique in Baton Rouge to pick out a second dress, they told her they still had her original dress in the back with her name on it. The dress should have been returned over a year earlier, but the lady in the store forgot to send it back. We truly believe that God was saving the dress because He knew that our story was not over, only delayed.

I share this part of our story to remind you that we don't always hear God perfectly and sometimes we inadvertently step off course. We can trust that when we do, God will draw us back. Hearing God and walking with Him is first and foremost about having a willing heart that is seeking to follow Him. As we seek to follow Him we analyze the data He gives us through His voice, His Word, His council through others and His peace in order to draw a conclusion on what He is saying and where He is leading.

What if God doesn't answer my questions?

I have learned over the years that although God desires a relationship with us, and wants us to ask Him questions and make requests, and wants to speak to us; He doesn't always give us the answers to the exact questions we are asking. There are a few reasons why God may choose not to answer your specific question:

- *One, your perspective of who He is could be wrong.* God is gracious and generous to His children, but He is not a genie who is there to grant your every wish or answer

What if God doesn't answer my questions? (cont.)

your question when you want to know it in the way you want to know it. The problem with the "God-as-heavenly-genie" concept is that we try to control Him—let Him out of His bottle when we need something, and put Him back when we don't.

- *Two, you are asking the wrong question.* "What numbers should I pick for the lottery?" Need I say more?

- *Three, your motives are not right.* James 4:3 says, "When you ask, you do not receive, because you ask with wrong motives, that you may spend what you get on your pleasures."

The Greek word translated as pleasures is *hēdonḗ* (that's where the word hedonism comes from), which has a strong connotation of satisfying selfish desires. Why would a loving heavenly Father give you something, or answer a question for something that is not ultimately good for you? Often times we don't even realize we have mixed motives when we ask or we don't realize that what we are asking for is actually not God's best for us.

- *Four, the timing is not right.* I believe this is the most common reason we don't get answers to our questions. God sees the bigger picture of the universe and your life. In theological terms we call that His omniscience—He

What if God doesn't answer my questions? (cont.)

sees and knows all! Your questions are based on your limited perspective. While your questions or requests may be valid, there may be other factors that you do not presently understand that need to fall in place before God answers.

- *Five, God is answering different questions.* We need to trust the mystery and sovereignty of God. Sometimes we are asking great questions and they are time sensitive, like praying for someone's healing yet we don't get a clear answer. I encourage you to continue to seek God while trying to not get frustrated about the apparent lack of an answer.

  Deuteronomy 29:29 says, "The secret things belong to the Lord our God, but the things revealed belong to us and to our sons forever, that we may observe all the words of this law." We can trust that God will make known to us what we need to know when we need to know it.

  If He doesn't answer your question, ask Him what He wants to say to you. Keep an open mind so that He can speak to you about any topic that is on His heart. Be willing to have Him challenge your motive and perspective, and even the question you are asking. Be open to the sources through which God will speak to you. He may be trying to answer your question, but do so in a way that is new to you.

HOW TO FIND PEACE

If you are in a place where you are in need of peace, or if you once had peace but you lost it, here are a few action steps that will help you find the supernatural peace that God desires to give you.

Pray

Be completely honest before God. He wants you to tell him what you are feeling anxious or unsure about and present your requests to Him. This is a necessary catalyst for the peace that Paul refers to in Philippians 4:6-7, "Do not be anxious about anything, but in every situation, by prayer and petition, with thanksgiving, present your requests to God. *And the peace of God, which transcends all understanding*, will guard your hearts and your minds in Christ Jesus." If you had peace previously, ask Him to help you retrace your steps back to that place, so you can release whatever you have picked up in the process that has made you question his guidance.

Release to God

This is typically the hardest, but the most important step. Sometimes it is called *laying it on the altar*, because you are fully releasing it to the Lord. When you have anxiety, pressure or stress, it is typically because you are still in control. A good litmus test to see if you have fully given something over to God is if you sense His peace after the release. If you are still experiencing restless nights and confusion, you are most likely still carrying the burden too much upon yourself. 1 Peter 5:6-7 instructs, "Humble yourselves, therefore, under God's mighty hand, that He may lift you up in due time. Cast all your anxiety on him because He cares for you." His care is always most obvious when your trust is at its fullest.

Trust God's Leadership

When you have given God full control, you can trust His leadership and His timing. God promises throughout His Word that He will guide you. Proverbs 3:5-6 says, "Trust in the Lord with all your heart and lean not on your own understanding; In all your ways submit to him, and He will make your paths straight." When you release what you had previously been holding onto, you will find not only does He flood you with His peace but new doors of opportunity open up. Why? Because He knows you can be trusted to trust Him again and again.

If you've asked God the questions on your heart, searched in His Word for answers to His questions or confirmation of what you believe He has spoken to you, and shared what you believe He is speaking to you with trusted counsel; hopefully you have experienced the final confirmation of peace about what He is saying. If not, don't be discouraged. Check out the text box in this chapter titled: What if God doesn't answer my questions? Wait until all the confirmations line up: His voice, His Word, His confirmation through trusted counsel and His peace.

If all the confirmations DID line up, then you are ready for Step Six in the practical science: Communicating Your Results.

CHAPTER FIVE | COMMUNICATING YOUR RESULTS

No experiment is complete without step six of the scientific method: communicating your results. For my science fair projects I created display boards that showed my hypothesis, research, experiments and the results. A professional scientist will publish their final report in a scientific journal, or present their findings at a scientific symposium.

For *Contact: The Practical Science of Hearing from God*, the final step is to tell someone what God has done in your life. As you listen for His voice, research His Word, listen to His counsel through others and experience a peace, or lack thereof, confirming what God was saying, then tell somebody! Let them know what God has done in your life, and encourage them that He can and will do the same in theirs. This is a critical part that is often missed.

YOUR TESTIMONY

One of the primary reasons I wrote this book was to remind you that God wants to speak to you and that He wants to move in your life. In the Old Testament the word testimony comes from the Hebrew root word *uwd,* which means "to repeat, return, or do it again." As you hear other people's testimonies of how God has moved in their life, you are reminded that your God is a God who loves to do it again. As you hear stories of God moving and bringing breakthrough in someone's life, your faith is strengthened to believe God is going to move in your life and bring breakthrough.

Revelation 19:10 states, "the testimony of Jesus is the Spirit of prophecy."[35] I believe every time we testify of God's goodness or share a testimony of how He has spoken to us or moved in our life; we are essentially prophesying to others what He wants to do in their life as they partner with Him. We are preparing the atmosphere for another move of God because testimony carries with it the power of change. If we speak out of our experience in God, we are not just giving information, but rather we are inviting others to believe that God will move again and that they too can experience the power of transformation.

This book contains numerous stories of how God has moved in my life and how hearing His voice has profoundly shaped and directed the course of my life. These testimonies continue to be a catalyst for faith and trust in my own walk with God because I am reminded how He has showed up for me time and time again. As I was writing these stories, I realized there are some updates to communicate about DC Metro's story. I am reminded of the wisdom of following His voice and how one step of obedience can set the course for years and years of good fruit if we stay connected to Him. This is the economy of God in action—any step of obedience on our part can be used to position us for the infinitely more He wants to do in and through us, as we align with His bigger purpose. So let me communicate the results of what God has done!

DC METRO'S TESTIMONY

Little did I know that saying "yes" to the vision to plant a life-giving church in the D.C. Metro area in 1998 would set the trajectory of my life to be a part of all the incredible blessings we have received as a church family. The ripple effect of that original "yes" has included: over ten thousand people committing their lives the Lord since 2007; countless other lives encountering God's goodness as marriages have been restored; people finding authentic community in what has been called one of the loneliest cities; and, many discovering how to hear His voice more clearly as they walk with Him towards their destiny.

As I have shared, it has not always been easy because God's timing has been very different than mine. In my mind, I was ready to move to D.C. to start a church in 1998. Looking back I'm very thankful that was not God's timing because in reality, I wasn't ready. I have found that God will often give you a vision years before He gives you the green light for the vision.

For example, I shared with you in chapter two that God gave me a vision for the property next door in 2010, but it has taken nearly five years for the door to open. It took almost two years for the car rental company that was leasing the building to move out—a move of God because they had been in the building for thirty years. It took another year and a half for our plans to be approved, and there were many times along the way where it looked like we were going to be denied access. All the while, I kept believing that God was going to bring it to pass at "an appointed time" (Hab. 2:3) and reminding myself "though it linger, wait for it, it will certainly come and not delay" (Hab. 2:3).

I am encouraged to share with you that DC Metro will be moving into this building located next door within approximately one month of the date that this book is launched. This building will allow us to double the number of seats available at our weekend services, allowing twice as many people in the D.C. Metro area the opportunity to encounter God in a real, relevant, and enjoyable environment. This will also allow us to turn our current sanctuary into a Children and Student Center, doubling our capacity to reach the next generation.

In chapter one, I told you about the vision God gave me in 2005 for seventeen campuses in the D.C. Metro area. I am excited to tell you we recently launched our third campus in Woodbridge, Virginia. God had clearly instructed us to take Virginia first. As we sought God on that phrase *Take Virginia First*, He helped me understand it further. I thought about the connotation of the word take and how it typically implies that it will not be an arduous battle to acquire. For example, when I hold a Lego car in my hand and tell my son Josiah to take it, all he has to do is step forward and grab it. Once I have instructed him to take it, he does not have to wrestle it out of my hands or convince me to give it to him. I had a similar sense about what God was saying for the next several campuses we would launch in Virginia. I believe God was telling us that as we continued to walk with Him, these campuses in Virginia would have His favor resting upon them. He would provide: the finances, the right location, the right leaders, and He would draw the people He desired to be a part of each campus.

Launching the first two campuses in Alexandria and Fairfax were more taxing and felt like an uphill battle, but we felt like we had the wind at our back when we launched the Woodbridge campus.

I believe this will be the case for the next several campuses we launch in Virginia, as we continue to heed His direction. This is a reminder that there are different seasons in God, and some are more challenging than others, but no matter what season you are in, it is important to stand on the word God has spoken to you.

In the beginning seasons of the church, I stood on the word I first received in 1998 reminding God that He called us to D.C. to plant a life-giving, multicultural church in the nation's capital. When we were experiencing difficulties finding a location to launch our second campus, year after year, I stood on the word that God had spoken that there would be seventeen campuses in the D.C. area and reminded Him that a multisite church was His idea. As we launched our third campus and now are in the process of looking for our fourth campus in Virginia, I regularly remind myself that He has commissioned us to *Take Virginia First,* and where He guides, He provides. The multisite vision is becoming a reality as we follow God's voice where He leads.

What has God spoken to you in previous seasons that you can stand on in this season? If you do not have anything that you know He spoke, spend some time this week listening for His voice and asking Him to lead you where He wants you to go. If it is still unclear, look at the desires that are in your heart and if they line up with God's Word and what you believe would please God, I encourage you to walk in that direction. As I mentioned earlier, if you keep your heart humble and your ear listening for His voice, He will redirect you if you ever step off course. I believe as you step out in faith with God, you are going to be amazed at His goodness. I am still astounded that He chose to use my life to plant DC Metro Church, and I believe as you continue to surrender to

Him, He wants to do something through your life that is even better than you can imagine.

MY PERSONAL TESTIMONY

At the beginning of this book I shared with you the story of miraculously being healed of cancer when I was a teenager. This year marks twenty-five years of being cancer-free! I hope that my testimony encourages you continue to seek God for any area of your life that needs healing or for anyone that you love who needs healing. I fully believe that God is a God who still heals today, and I pray that my testimony will be a catalyst to continue to contend for full healing and wholeness in every area of your life.

I share all of this to encourage you to pray for breakthrough in whatever ailment, illness, or disease in your body or of someone you love. I am often asked why God does not heal in every situation, and while I cannot fully answer that question, I can tell you that those who choose to believe and pray for healing see breakthrough at a much higher rate than those who don't. We are wise to choose to focus on what God is doing rather than focusing on what He is not doing. God is a God of hope, and you never know when your breakthrough could come, so I encourage you to keep seeking Him and to keep your heart alive to Him.

I have also seen incredible breakthroughs in my marriage and family. Although Taryn and I have been in love since we first started dating seventeen years ago, we have walked through some challenging seasons in our marriage and in our calling. The pressure of leading a growing church and family is real, and we were not immune to the weight of these struggles. Taryn received a prophetic word years before we were married that although she had grown up in a broken home, she would have a happy marriage and a happy family life. We named our home *the Happy Nest* as a prophetic declaration of the word that was spoken over her. We have stood upon this word as we both worked hard to have a happy, healthy marriage and to raise our kids to have an authentic love for Jesus in a home where they can grow into who God is calling them to be.

Taryn threw me a surprise birthday party for my fortieth birthday a few months ago. During the party I was reflecting on God's goodness in our lives. I am encouraged to share with you that our marriage is as strong as it has ever been, and I am more in love with my wife than I was when she walked down the aisle to me thirteen years ago. Our three boys, Isaac, Josiah, and Asher are full of energy and life, and Karis is our little princess. They have each brought us indescribable joy, as they, along with Taryn, are the best presents Jesus has ever given me. I am excited to see what God has for us as a family as we continue the incredible adventure of following His voice.

Is there a relationship in your life you are praying for? Maybe you are single and you are wondering if you are ever going to meet the right person. Perhaps you are in a difficult season in your marriage or one of children is walking through a significant struggle. Maybe there is relational discord with someone you love and you do not know how to reconcile the relationship. Whatever the relational challenge you are experiencing, know that God wants to walk through the challenge with you. I encourage you to be one that chooses hope in each of these situations believing that they can be reversed.

This book contains testimonies about what happened when Taryn and I surrendered our life to the Lord. The testimonies are of different ways that God has spoken to me, Taryn, and others about our personal decisions and about the greater vision that he had for us and DC Metro Church. You may not be called to do the same things I have done, but be assured God has a purpose for your life. Your sphere of influence may be different than mine, but God can do incredible things through your surrendered life as you continue to say "yes" to the adventure of being led by the Lord's voice!

As you position yourself to hear from Him, preparing to enter into the forty-day experiment challenge, remember to communicate your results as you hear God's voice and experience Him moving in your life. As I hope me sharing my results has been an encouragement to you, God wants to use you to encourage someone else, and invite them on a similar journey to know Him more!

PART THREE

THE EXPERIMENT: A GUIDE TO HEARING GOD'S VOICE

I n part one of this book, I said *"Contact: The Practical Science of Hearing from God* is written to help believers discover and apply specific knowledge to the practical dilemma of wanting to hear clearly from Him so that we can experience more depth in our relationship with Him."* Throughout this book, I have explored ways that you can position yourself to encounter the supernatural voice and leadings of God—make contact with Him.

You started by asking God a question(s), and creating space and time in your life to hear from Him (Step One of the scientific method: Ask a Question). You learned about the still, small voice of God, and some of the different ways He will communicate with you.

You learned how to do background research taking your question(s) and researching what the Word of God says about the topic (Step Two of the scientific method: Do Background Research). You are now familiar with the S.O.A.P. method of Bible study and the GOD SPA.

As you listen for His *still, small voice* and research the Word of God, it should lead you to a hypothesis of what you believe God is speaking to you (Step Three of the scientific method: Construct a Hypothesis). Next you share what you believe God is speaking to you with trusted friends or counselors—testing to see if they confirm what you are hearing (Step Four of the scientific method: Test Your Hypothesis).

After this, you analyze what you have heard through His voice, His Word, His counsel through others, and see if your conclusion is confirmed by His peace (Step Five of the scientific method: Analyze Your Data and Draw a Conclusion). Finally, you tell others what you have learned through this process and what God has done in your life (Step Six of the scientific process: Communicate Your Results).

I have shared different ways that God speaks and shared stories of learning to recognize His voice, but the real purpose of this book is for you to hear God for yourself.

THE EXPERIMENT

I challenge you to commit to the experiment I mentioned in the beginning of the book—a forty-day challenge designed to help you hear God and grow closer to Him. We have created a workbook called *The Experiment—40 Days of Hearing God's Voice Workbook* that contains a forty-day devotional that will help you implement the practices in this book and position yourself to hear from God!

The experiment challenge is for you to practically apply what you have learned by spending thirty minutes each day in prayer and Bible study for the next forty days. I believe that God will meet you as you step out to seek Him. The promise of His guidance is right there in Psalm 32:8, "I will instruct you and teach you in the way you should go. I will guide you with my eye."[36] There is no more important skill to gain to walk into everything that God has for you than learning to recognize and follow His voice.

Before you jump into the actual workbook, I want to share some practical instructions on how to have a devo time. Whenever I am coaching anyone on how to hear from God, I encourage them to focus on including five areas into their devo time with God. I have yet to have someone come back to me and say that they have not experienced a significant increase in being able to hear and discern the voice of God in their life. At the end of the instructions, is a short commitment for you to read and sign acknowledging your desire to commit to the forty-day experiment.

STEP ONE: PICK A TIME AND A PLACE TO MEET WITH GOD.

Before Taryn and I moved to Washington D.C. to plant DC Metro Church, I had been drawn to this area for many years because I knew it was a city of influence. If you can influence the D.C. area for Christ, you can influence the nation, and ultimately you will influence the world. Movers and shakers are attracted to D.C., and the people here tend to have an obsession with schedules and appointments. On more than one occasion, I have heard someone say something to the effect of, "I have an opening three weeks from now for thirty minutes. Sorry, everything else is booked solid."

I have heard these same people confess that they struggle to find time to meet with God. My thought in pastoring them has been simple, *How is it that we prioritize meetings with people we don't even like and neglect to meet with the God that we love?* I don't say this in a critical way, but rather as a wakeup call and a reminder that we prioritize what we value. I challenge you to pull out your iPhone or your Day-Timer right now and schedule daily time with God.

This sounds simple, but it is all too easy to let the appointment slip if you do not tenaciously guard it. In my earlier years I was more sporadic in my devo times, but I found that missed appointments with God led to disappointments in life. How can I expect to find the abundant life He offers if I am not seeking Him each day to guide me into His fullness?

The Time:

I recommend that you choose the time when you are at your very best. I believe that God always gives us His very best, so I want to respond in suit by spending time with Him when I am most alert and ready to receive. Some people like getting up early, like five a.m.—that's great for them, but I am not at my best that early. I have found that God does not speak to me at that hour because...well, I am asleep (He can speak to me in my dreams if He wants to say anything to me before the sun rises). God is happy to meet with you any time of day, so what time works for you?

The Place:

Next find a place for you and God to meet. I recommend going somewhere that you love. When I take Taryn out on a date, I do not go to a fast food restaurant because I want it to be a place that we both love and enjoy going to together. My organic, gluten-free-loving wife's love language is most certainly not some greasy French fries or being in an environment with screaming kids and dirty booths. Instead I try to choose a healthy restaurant that has atmosphere where we are able to connect with each other.

In a similar way, I recommend choosing a place for your time with God that you are excited to go to and a place that is conducive to connecting with Him. In my previous house, I would walk the streets in the neighborhood and pray. I am sure my neighbors wondered what I was doing, *Who is this guy who paces the streets late at night in dark clothing talking to himself?*

I decided when we moved to our new house that I didn't want to scare my neighbors or make them think I am any crazier than they probably already do, so I chose a new prayer strategy. Now I meet with God every day in my basement or in a special chair on my back porch overlooking the water, rolling hills, and the beautiful country landscape. It reminds me of where I grew up as a boy in Louisiana and helps me disconnect from the fast pace of the city, so I can hear from Him.

If you are not able to be out in nature, I recommend preparing a place that you can make sacred. It could be a chair in a quiet room. It could even be your bed (if you can resist the temptation of dozing off). The most important part of choosing a place is that when you are there for your appointment with God, you can be fully present. Whenever I sit in my chair, I don't look at my phone or answer emails. It is time solely focused on Him and what He has to say. It is my best and my favorite meeting of the day.

I believe that God loves to come to places that are especially prepared for Him. It is our way to honor Him and demonstrate how excited we are for Him to come. In Exodus, the Lord tells Moses to tell the people to prepare for His coming. Exodus 19:10-11 says, "Go to the people and consecrate them today and tomorrow. Have them wash their clothes and be ready by the third day, because on that day the Lord will come down on Mount Sinai in the sight of all the people."

On the third morning, there was thunder, lightning, and a thick cloud over the mountain. God showed up in a spectacular way in response to His people's preparation to hear from Him. There was a trumpet blast before Moses spoke. Then God answered. I don't know about you but my devo times are not usually quite this dramatic, but I have found when I prepare a time and a place to meet with Him, He shows up.

There is a classic eighties flick that I love called *Field of Dreams*. The movie is about an Iowa farmer that hears a voice telling him, "If you build it, he will come." Although in the movie it is referring to building a baseball field for the Chicago Black Sox, I have found this principle to be true in my relationship with God. If you will prepare a place for Him and build in time to be with Him, He will show up. If you build it, He will come! Once you have picked a time and a place, what do you do next?

STEP TWO: BE STILL AND WORSHIP.

Psalm 46:10 says to "be still and know that I am God." Honestly, I am not always good at being still. I would definitely rather be moving, preferably at a very high speed. Fortunately, the Hebrew word for the phrase <u>be still</u> is *raphah*, which is not necessarily a literal stillness but more of a stillness of the soul. Psalm 46:10 can be translated as, "Stop striving and know that I am God." The context of this passage was at a time when Israel was being threatened by other nations. In the midst of these threats, they could trust in the covenant that God made with them and know that He would be their very present help, refuge, and strength (see Psalm 46:1).

There is something about being still before God that reminds us we are not in charge—He is. Once we are still before Him, we can enter into true worship. I have found that when I worship, everything shifts. If my perspective was off, I see rightly once again. I am reminded of the bigness of God and of how much He loves me and how much I love Him. I am also reminded again of how much I need Him and how trustworthy He is.

I have not always begun my devo times with worship, but I highly recommend taking some time to worship before you jump into reading the Word. Worship helps you release burdens you are carrying and shifts your perspective so you see rightly again. Sometimes I will put a song on repeat, so that the words wash over me again and again. Our hearts are tenderized in His presence. We were made to worship.

It is during my time of being still and worshipping that I often bring my questions to God (Step one of the scientific method). As I am still before Him, and aware of His presence, my heart open to Him—I share with Him what is on my heart.

STEP THREE: READ AND PRAY.

God has written down His opinions and wisdom regarding the most common problems we face, so I recommend spending time looking at what He says in His Word—step two of the scientific method. There is an integral partnership between the Word and the Spirit when it comes to God speaking. As you open your Bible and read, you are hearing what God has already spoken and asking the Holy Spirit to make it come alive so you can discern what God IS SPEAKING to you.

In chapter two, I gave you some basic Bible study tools that have worked in my personal devos. We have included a daily passage from the Bible for each of your forty days that is found in *The Experiment—40 Days of Hearing God's Voice Workbook.*

After you complete the experiment, we recommend you trying one of the following options.

1. *A topical study:* Take one of the questions that you have been asking God or a question that He has already answered. Look for what the Bible has to say around that question or issue. For example: if you are asking God's direction on marriage, search out in a concordance or in an online search those passages in the Bible that deal with marriage. If you are asking Him for wisdom on some decisions you have to make, what does the Bible say about wisdom? Your study will often either confirm something He has already spoken, or it will direct you to your question's answer.
2. *A book or character study:* Choose a book of the Bible to study, or choose a person from the Bible to study.

Since the experiment is to spend thirty minutes a day with God, I recommend you start by spending ten to fifteen of those minutes in study after you worship. As you get into the Word, that time will likely increase. Sometimes I study for hours looking up Greek and Hebrew words and cross referencing passages in the Bible. Other times I spend just a few minutes reading a few verses.

Sometimes I feel as though God is speaking directly to me through His Word, and I understand exactly what He is asking me to do next through something I read. Other times when I read, God feels abstract and I struggle to understand how the passage has any correlation to my life whatsoever. This is very normal. Keep reading. As you continue to read with your ears and heart open, He will speak to you.

I believe that reading the Word is meant to be an interactive experience—God wants you to dialogue with Him as you are reading, so I recommend praying as you are reading and praying after you read. I often ask Him what He means in certain passages or how I can apply certain wisdom that I read to my current situations. The Word of God was never meant to be merely moral instructions but rather a launch pad into interacting with God, so if you are not talking to God as you read, you are missing the point.

After you finish reading, take a few minutes to respond in prayer to what you read. Pray about whatever is on your heart—those questions from step one of the scientific method. Many people lose traction in prayer because they think they need to be praying about major world issues. If those big topics are on your heart, go for it, but if you are distracted by the fight you just had with your significant other or your friend, pray about that first. Maybe you are struggling with feeling overwhelmed by all your responsibilities at work or home and the weight you have gained recently from stress eating or with feeling like you can't make traction in your finances. Pray about what is on your heart. God desires authenticity more than manufactured piety.

Often when I am trying to pray for more than a minute or two my mind starts to wander. When that happens I have found it extremely helpful to write down my prayers. This brings us to the next step in how we can practically position ourselves to hear the supernatural voice of God.

STEP FOUR: LISTEN AND WRITE.

I recently heard that the above average listener only listens for approximately seventeen seconds without diverting the conversation back to themselves. It seems that we are just naturally egocentric unless we intentionally guard against it. To illustrate this point, when you see a group picture, who is the first person you look at? What criteria do you use to determine if you like the picture—how your friend looks, or whether the angle is flattering for the person next to you? I didn't think so.

In our relationship with God and with others, most of us struggle with being good listeners, but we will miss many important promptings from God if we do not take the time to listen for "the still, small voice of God" (1 Kings 19:12)[37]. Do you pause to listen to God or do you spend most of your time rattling off prayer requests?

Prayer is meant to be a two-way conversation. I know some people get frustrated when they hear pastors and teachers say that because they struggle to hear from God when they stop to listen, so they just keep talking.

This wrestling can come from many places, and it is important to discern its root so that you can address it. It could be from a place of doubt—some people don't believe He is really going to speak to them or trust that they can discern His voice. Other times it can come from wrong teaching—some people have been taught in

Christian churches today that He does not speak to us personally, so they don't even try. It can also come from fear—some people have stopped trying to listen to what He is saying because they are fearful of what He might ask them to do. It could even be busyness—some of us don't stop and listen simply because we are always on the run.

If you struggle to listen, what is the root motive? Confess this to God and ask Him to help you take time to listen, believing that He wants to talk with you and that whatever He asks is for your ultimate good.

Two-way Journaling:

As I shared in chapter two, the single most revolutionary step I have taken in the past several years to dramatically increase both the amount of time I spend listening AND the frequency I hear from God is something I call two-way journaling. To refresh your memory, go back and review that section in chapter two.

You first write God an honest and authentic letter, thank Him for who He is, release any burdens, ask Him questions or invite Him to speak into your life situations or problems. Then, write yourself a letter from God. He may encourage you, or bring scriptures to your mind that deal with your struggles or questions. When you finish journaling, submit everything back to God, ask Him to make clear or redirect you in what you heard. Test everything with the same filters you do any time you are attempting to hear from God.

You will have an opportunity to try two-way journaling as a part of your devotional time in the workbook. If this is a new exercise for you, I believe you will enjoy this focused way of processing with the Lord and hearing what He says as you write!

STEP FIVE: SHARE AND OBEY.

Who can you share what God spoke to you? If it is direction you received, it is wise to share this with the godly counsel in your life. As I shared in chapter three, I am committed to always having close, godly counsel in my life and have given them permission to speak into my life and hold me accountable.

After you have shared with godly counsel in your life in order to seek their direction and accountability, ask God if there is anyone else He wants you to tell about what He has done or how He has met you. If it is a revelation or insight He has showed you, think about who could benefit from hearing what God has been teaching you. Is there someone in your life going through something similar that might be encouraged by your story or what God spoke to you?

I encourage you to be ready to tell whomever God brings in your path, even if it is a stranger you meet on an airplane or someone who is a casual acquaintance. Dr. Umidi, one of DC Metro's overseers, talks about how God loves to use us as "UPS men" because He has special delivery packages for divine appointments in our life. This special delivery package could be you telling the story of something God just walked you through or a revelation God shared with you in your devo time. As you walk in step with the Holy Spirit, He will highlight exactly who and what to share. Will you step out in obedience?

As a final step in the process, spend some time asking God if there are any additional steps of obedience or action steps He would like you to take. Or if there is something He has already showed you to do, commit to walking that out and commit to the time frame you will need to complete it. Colossians 3:15 reminds us to let God's peace lead us when we feel challenged to obey or step out because His peace is a tangible reminder of His presence with us.

As you begin to use *The Experiment—40 Days of Hearing God's Voice Workbook* note that I structured it after the devo format above that I personally follow. For me the scientific method steps that I talked about in the earlier chapters fit well into the devo format. Get ready to hear from God and be amazed at all He has for you, as you position yourself before Him and incline your ear to His voice!

THE COMMITMENT

I included this simple commitment between you and God, because I believe your commitment to the experiment will radically change your life. Read it, decide if you are ready to take the plunge, and sign and date. (It is recommended that you use The Experiment—40 Days of Hearing God's Voice Workbook to complete the commitment, as the Bible passages and steps to devo are already created for you!)

My Commitment to God!

I have read and understand the basic steps to hearing the voice of God introduced in Contact: The Practical Science of Hearing from God. I am excited at the opportunity to develop my relationship to God, learning how to spend time in His presence and Word, and growing in my ability to hear from Him. I consider it an honor that God desires to communicate with me, and an adventure of learning how to make contact with Him!

I recognize that my desire to know Him needs an investment of my time and discipline. Therefore, for the next forty days, I commit to the following:

1. *I will purposely position myself to hear from God, picking a time and place to daily meet with Him.*

2. *I will follow the suggested devo format Pastor David introduced: spending time in stillness and worship, reading the Word of God, prayer and two-way journaling.*

3. *I will find a trusted friend or friends to serve as godly counsel, and share what I am learning and believe God is speaking to me.*

4. *Finally, I will step out in obedience and do whatever He calls me to do including sharing with others what God is doing in my life.*

I recognize that my commitment for the next forty days is the start of a new dimension in my relationship with God, and the principles that I put into practice during this time will lay the foundation for a lifelong experience of making contact with God!

_____   _____
My Signature   **Date**

FREE RESOURCES

Send an email to resources@contactexperiment.com or visit http://ContactExperiment.com/resources to receive these bonuses:

- "Using Contact in Your Daily Life": An exclusive interview with Dr. Stine on how he applies the principles of *Contact* on a daily basis, and how you can too.

- "Contact, The Practical Science of Hearing from God": Exclusive video sermon presented by Dr. Stine.

ABOUT THE AUTHOR

Pastor David and Taryn Stine

As Lead Pastor of DC Metro Church, Dr. David Stine is known for his practical biblical teaching, his visionary leadership, and his heart to impact the D.C. Metropolitan area. David's authenticity and his ability to communicate the truth of God's Word in a humorous, dynamic, and revelatory manner helps people understand the Bible and how to apply its teachings to their everyday lives.

David is passionate about people coming to know Christ, getting planted in God's house, and becoming transformational leaders who work together to build a God-first culture throughout the D.C. Metro area. He is honored to be teaching, training, and coaching church leaders and future church planters because he believes that the local church is the hope of the world and that we are meant to be relationally connected with other leaders.

Shortly after coming to Christ in college, David knew there was a call on his life to full-time ministry and sensed God leading him to seminary at Regent University, where he earned his Masters Degree (M.A.) in Practical Theology and his Doctoral Degree (D.Min) in Leadership.

David met his future wife Taryn at Louisiana State University where they both majored in Business and were involved in a campus ministry together. After graduation, they were advancing in their respective careers, but the deepest desire of their hearts was to "do something great for God" together.

Today they are parents to four growing children and loving their call to full-time ministry at DC Metro. They believe nothing compares to the joy of experiencing the transformation in people's lives as they choose the God-first life.

CONTACT THE AUTHOR

If you have any comments or encouragement after reading this book, we would love to hear from you. You can contact Pastor David at contact@dcmetro.org.

ENDNOTES

1 From https://www.barna.org/barna-update/culture/364-americans-feel-connected-to-jesus#.Va_CtIr3anN

2 The Holy Bible, New King James Version, Copyright © 1982 by Thomas Nelson, Inc.

3 Frank C. Laubach, *Channels of Spiritual Power*. (New York: Fleming H. Revell Co., 1954.), 92.

4 Holy Bible, New Living Translation copyright © 1996, 2004, 2007, 2013 by Tyndale House Foundation. Used by permission of Tyndale House Publishers Inc., Carol Stream, Illinois 60188. All rights reserved. New Living, NLT, and the New Living Translation logo are registered trademarks of Tyndale House Publishers.

5 From http://www.quotes.net/quote/9306

6 Sylvia Earle. (n.d.). BrainyQuote.com. Retrieved October 20, 2014, from BrainyQuote.com Web site: http://www.brainyquote.com/quotes/authors/s/sylvia_earle.html

7 Thomas Berger. (n.d.). BrainyQuote.com. Retrieved October 20, 2014, from BrainyQuote.com Web site: http://www.brainyquote.com/quotes/authors/t/thomas_berger.html

8 Yancey quoting Eckhart in *Reaching for the Invisible God: What Can We Expect to Find?* Phillip Yancey.

9 From http://www.thegospelcoalition.org/article/20-quotes-from-new-book-on-prayer

10 Gerhard Freidrich, ed. *Theological Dictionary of the New Testament*. Vol. 5 (Grand Rapids: WM. B. Eerdmans Co., 1967.), 774-775.

11 Thoralf Gilbrant, ed. *The New Testament Greek-English Dictionary.* (Springfield: The Complete Bible Library Co., 1986), 630.

12 Ibid, 385.

13 From www.thinkexist.com

14 Ibid

15 The Holy Bible, King James Version, Public Domain.

16 The Holy Bible, New King James Version, Copyright © 1982 by Thomas Nelson, Inc.

17 A. W. Tozer, *The Pursuit of God.* (Christian Publications, 1948.), 10.

18 From http://www.enewhope.org/nextsteps/journaling/

19 Enrico Fermi. (n.d.). BrainyQuote.com. Retrieved October 29, 2014, from BrainyQuote.com Web site: http://www.brainyquote .com/quotes/authors/e/enrico_fermi.html

20 The Holy Bible, New King James Version, Copyright © 1982 by Thomas Nelson, Inc.

21 Ibid.

22 Peter Hass, *Q&A—Church Size, "What is the Ideal church size?" as well as "How do you define 'church'?" "What is the perfect church format?"* Retrieved from http://www.substancechurch .com/sites/default/files/QA-ChurchSize.pdf

23 Finerman, W., Tisch, S., Starkey, S., Newirth, C. (Producers), & Zemeckis, R (Director). (July 6, 1994). *Forest Gump* [Motion picture]. United States of America: Paramount.

24 Larry Crabb, *The Safest Place on Earth.* (Nashville, TN: Word, 1999), 22.

25 C.S. Lewis, *Letters to Malcolm: Chiefly on Prayer.* (San Diego: Harvest, 1964), 93.

26 C.S. Lewis. (n.d.) Goodreads.com. Retrieved June 19, 2015, from Goodreads.com Web site: http://www.goodreads.com /quotes/183419-in-friendship-we-think-we-have-chosen-our-peers-in-reality

27 From http://www.brainyquote.com/quotes/authors/m /milton_friedman.html#DQzdzAc8qgiLPLMf.99

28 The Franklin Institute, www.fi.edu

29 The Lemison Center, www.invention.smithsonain.org

30 The Franklin Institute, www.fi.edu

31 Ibid.

32 William Barclay, *The New Daily Study Bible.* (Westminster John Knox Press, March 1, 2004).

33 International Standard Bible Encyclopedia, http://www .studylight.org/encyclopedias/isb/

34 The Holy Bible, New King James Version, Copyright © 1982 by Thomas Nelson, Inc.

35 Ibid.

36 Ibid.

37 The Holy Bible, King James Version, Public Domain.

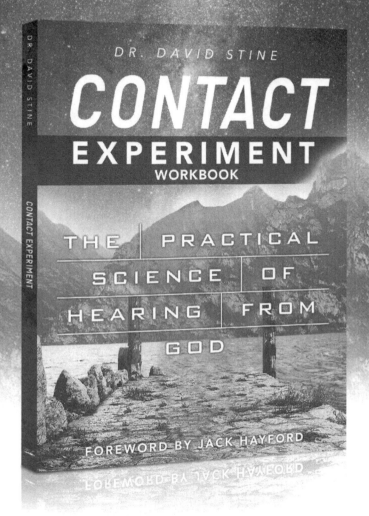

23903115R00091

Made in the USA
Middletown, DE
07 September 2015